Dear You

BE AT YOUR BEST,
IMPROVE YOUR BEST,
AND
INFLUENCE THE REST.

RED KERUSSO

ISBN 978-1-64471-391-4 (Paperback)
ISBN 978-1-64471-392-1 (Digital)

Copyright © 2019 Red Kerusso
All rights reserved
First Edition

All rights reserved. No part of this publication may be reproduced, distributed, or transmitted in any form or by any means, including photocopying, recording, or other electronic or mechanical methods without the prior written permission of the publisher. For permission requests, solicit the publisher via the address below.

Covenant Books, Inc.
11661 Hwy 707
Murrells Inlet, SC 29576
www.covenantbooks.com

This is for you, Christy, my soulmate, my precious wife! For when my earthly time is gone, you, our loved ones and world will, forever, have letters from my heart to remind you that you're never alone! Your encouragement and support led the way...for, without your love and support, this would not have happened and our legacy would not be! Thank you, Thank you for all your selfless support and unconditional love and for simply being you! P.S. I love you the most!

Dear you,

Amidst life's trials, it's human nature to look for answers or a way out. In fact, throughout these trials, it's natural to feel trapped and/or full of doubt. Hold on, never quit and never give up, for there is a way out! You see, the natural response is to worry, run, escape; however, the spiritual nature enables you to endure through the trial. How? Because your spiritual nature knows that He, being GOD, will make a way! When it seems like you are all alone and no one cares, your spiritual nature knows that He is right there with you. Just like the trial at the Red Sea, where the people felt like nowhere else to go and Pharaoh's army was closing in, God showed up and showed out; He rolled back the water and made a way out of the trial! So no matter what you are facing, battling, or going through, know that you are not alone. He shows up right on time and makes the way! I am praying that whatever you are facing for God's hand to show up and show out, making the way! God bless you!

Love, Red

Dear you,

LET THE DICE ROLL! The dice of life roll even when you want to hold; after all, perseverance isn't strengthened without obstacles to overcome. Proverbs 16:33 says, "We may throw the dice, but the Lord determines how they fall." I encourage you, no matter where the dice fall, to consistently trust Him and overcome the obstacles. Yes, at times, we might think that where the dice fall isn't fair and want to walk away from the game; however, we have no earthly weights or scales to measure God's plans for our lives, which means you trust Him, believing that He has a perfect will for you. In fact, a solid Proverb found in 16:11 says, "The Lord demands accurate scales and balances; He sets the standards for fairness." So wherever the dice fall, there is a plan for you and a fair standard set by God for each of us to uphold. Stay solid, ready, and strong, as the DICE OF LIFE ROLL! God bless you.

Love, Red

Dear you,

If you wait until you can do everything for everybody, instead of something for somebody, you'll end up doing nothing for nobody; selfless leadership starts with helping one. Let your journey not only show your love, but also how selfless you are. I'm reminded of Philippians 2:1–11, a passage on selflessness; verse 4 says, "Let each of you look not only to his own interests, but also to the interests of others." Seek to be more selfless in life and start by helping one. God bless you!

Love, Red

DEAR YOU

Dear you,

Hold on to those irreplaceable tools, such as wisdom, knowledge, integrity, and honor; for the right tools build the right legacy. Use those tools in your life living for Jesus; after all, Jesus's death on the Cross, followed by His resurrection, gives you life along with the tools needed to survive. He loves you so much. God bless you.

Love, Red

Dear you,

Leaders, stand ready—ready to transform the future. You want strength? You want unity with the right core values? Then you have to establish authentic vision, founded on honesty, while keeping a growth mindset built upon seamless integrity. At the end of the day, it's about transformation evidenced by hard work. Sometimes you have to rejuvenate your relationships, allowing each other to leverage core strengths. Be aware that, at times, the ones that appear to be the weakest link might be the strongest, holding it all together for the bigger picture. Psalm 28:7a says, "The Lord is my strength and shield. I trust him with all my heart." Allow Him to strengthen you and the team, as you carry out the mission of fulfilling an authentic God vision! God bless you!

Love, Red

Dear you,

Wobbly bridges are far more salvageable than burnt ones; for wobbly bridges just might be able to be repaired. Hence the importance of choosing your method of demolition wisely, for some methods lead to permanent destruction. Take a moment to read 1 Corinthians 3:9–15. Are you building on the right foundation, as well as up to code when making required repairs?

Love, Red

Dear you,

The courage to encourage, something we each should proudly be known to do, but is hard…especially when you, yourself, are feeling down! That's right, let's keep it real, sometimes we let folks pass on by because we are not feeling encouraged ourselves. A solid Proverb found in 12:25 says, "Worry weighs a person down; an encouraging word cheers a person up." I encourage you to stop worrying and find a way to reach out and encourage someone…it might even be yourself. Why? Because encouraging words not only impact lives, but can also be what saves a life. Strive to always be at your best as you influence the rest. I'm praying for you; may God touch and impact your life and may He provide full restoration of your courage so that you might never cease to encourage those that cross your path. God bless you.

Love, Red

Dear you,

When the rain pours, cleaning and washing away life's dirt and grime, I'm reminded of when God reigns, His forgiveness washes away life's internal dirt and grime. First John 1:9 says, "If we confess our sins, He is faithful and just to forgive us our sins and to cleanse us from all unrighteousness." Let God reign and experience His life cleansing rain. God bless you.

Love, Red

DEAR YOU

Dear you,

You might not have everything you want, but God gives you everything you need. Philippians 4:19 says, "And my God will supply every need of yours according to His riches in glory in Christ Jesus." I encourage you, trust Him to fulfill your needs. He will show you the way. God bless you.

Love, Red

Dear you,

You, YES, YOU are a somebody! How do you define your self-worth? Do you consider yourself priceless? If not, start now. Believe in yourself, hold your head up, shoulders back and believe that you're priceless; after all, you were bought by the blood of Christ Jesus. First Corinthians 7:23a says, "God paid a high price for you!" WOW! Even when you feel like a nobody, you're always a somebody to God.

Love, Red

Dear you,

Set a solid course—a course that grows strong roots. Jeremiah 17:7–8 describes a person we all should strive to be; it says, "But blessed are those who trust in the Lord and have made the Lord their hope and confidence. They are like trees planted along a riverbank, with roots that reach deep into the water. Such trees are not bothered by the heat or worried by long months of drought. Their leaves stay green, and they never stop producing fruit." So are you on the right track? If not, you can be; up to you to change course and plant your roots in the right soil.

Love, Red

Dear you,

Be careful what you say, for your word, apart from your heart, is one of your most valuable assets. I encourage you to never compromise your word. Be a leader known to have the word as solid as a rock, rather than a word sticky and slick as sinking sand. Abraham Lincoln once said, "Better to remain silent and be thought a fool than to speak out and remove all doubt." I leave you with a solid Proverb found in 13:3, which says, "Those who control their tongue will have a long life; opening your mouth can ruin everything." Be careful what you say. God bless you!

Love, Red

Dear you,

Humility precedes honor. You see, when you lead self and/or a team, humility builds up and strengthens, whereas pride causes your fall. I have seen many leaders along the way that are self-consumed, the pompous type. Their empire, their legacy eventually came crashing down, destroyed because of pretentious approaches rather than the humble approach of building up and aligning the team to operate as one. Confucius was noted to say, "Humility is the solid foundation of all virtues." Is your foundation solid? What about your honor? I encourage you to seek out wisdom, stay humble and don't settle for good be GREAT; be honorable! Proverbs 15:33 says, "Fear of the Lord teaches wisdom; humility precedes honor." God bless you!

Love, Red

DEAR YOU

Dear you,

You are the gardener of your life—up to you to prune away the bad to stimulate the new. A wise gardener pays attention because seasons change and required pruning is accomplished, as the old fades away. The reward found in pruning is when the new season arrives new life buds from the tree. Yesterday's actions prepared you for today and today is an opportunity to prune and purge the failures for a new and successful tomorrow. Are you diligently pruning? John 15:1–2 says, "I am the true grapevine, and my Father is the gardener. He cuts off every branch of mine that doesn't produce fruit, and he prunes the branches that do bear fruit so they will produce even more." God bless you!

Love, Red

Dear you,

There are times in life when you'll face uncertainty; regardless of "what" is affecting you, your life is not falling apart it's falling into place. From my experience, some of your biggest moments of breakthrough happen during your most uncertain times. Proverbs 3:5–6 says, "Trust in the Lord with all your heart; do not depend on your own understanding. Seek His will in all you do, and He will show you which path to take." So in any situation, trust and know that God has a plan in and through it. God bless you.

Love, Red

Dear you,

You know those folks that come up to you at restaurants, your local Walmart or gas station asking for some money or food? How often do you offer to buy them some food or gas? A solid Proverb found in 19:17 says, "If you help the poor, you are lending to the Lord—and He will repay you!" I encourage you not to be so quick to dismiss them. After all, what if they are angels as Hebrews 13:2 says, "Don't forget to show hospitality to strangers, for some who have done this have entertained angels without realizing it." The point is to help others along the way, as you show the realness of God through your actions. God bless you.

Love, Red

Dear you,

Today is the beginning of many new opportunities, not only to finalize old issues, but to continue, or begin, new and emerging requirements. Consider the sun rise and sun set, both consistently hit the horizon dead on. Even when clouds cover the view, the sun still rises and sets. Be encouraged to be precise in all your actions and never let the clouds of life hinder your progress at reaching your goals. Keep your head and eyes set on the mark, approaching life with Philippians 3:14 applied, "I press on to reach the end of the race and receive the heavenly prize for which God, through Christ Jesus, is calling us." God bless you and may you and your life shine in all aspects!

Love, Red

DEAR YOU

Dear you,

Every road you've taken has led to today. Yes, at times, those roads were tough, but you're still standing; you do your best to hold it all together, even when the struggle is real and appears to have no end. Yes, you do, and will have, moments where you think you are going strong and then, BAM, life just knocks you down to the ground. So what sets you apart? Your character and strength, for they shine at your lowest moments. It's in those moments, where you are barely hanging on to the little you have left, but remain strong when others fall weak, that you shine the brightest. I encourage you to be reminded that even the smallest steps in life have purpose, and, with each step, stay committed in resting and waiting on the Lord. Psalm 37:16 says, "A little that a righteous man hath is better than the riches of many wicked." Keep on keeping on because you're held in the hand of God. God bless you!

Love, Red

Dear you,

A wise person knows that perceptions change, realities evolve. See beyond what you can see; open your inner eyes. Are you facing a strenuous situation? Maybe it's a situation with another person, maybe it's a decision that tremendously affects your future, or maybe it's righting a wrong. Whatever the "MAYBE" is to you, you can succeed. In 1 Samuel 17, we recount the remarkable story of David and Goliath. David was a scrawny young boy and Goliath was an overall superior strength kind of guy; we all know both types. Goliath just knew he would win, but David knew he had God. David didn't just say he would fight him, he said he would KILL HIM. Verse 46 says, "Today the Lord will conquer you, and I will kill you and cut off your head. And then I will give the dead bodies of your men to the birds and wild animals, and the whole world will know that there is a God in Israel!" I encourage you to stand up against your personal Goliaths, see beyond what you can physically see and show that God is ALIVE AND REAL! Stand ready; God bless you!

Love, Red

Dear you,

Just because you can, doesn't mean you should. Like said many times before, consider those second and third order effects; for these effects stimulate actions. Do the actions coincide with what you believe? Hmmm. Reminds me of Bo Bennett who said, "Think before you act and act on what you believe." In other words, your actions not only influence reactions, but also follow and/or represent you. I encourage each of us to stay wise and think before we act or speak, because words can't be reeled in and actions are, at times, not forgotten. I leave you with a solid Proverb found in 13:16, which says, "Wise people think before they act; fools don't—and even brag about their foolishness." Stay solid, make a difference. God bless you.

Love, Red

DEAR YOU

Dear you,

Emotions are in the world of your life; the way to negotiate an emotion is to abandon weakness, while embracing inner strength. Strength to control your innermost heart impacts how your emotions take life; for the output of emotions is usually what's hiding in your deepest deep of heart. I encourage each of us to strengthen our deepest innermost self, flush out the negative and strengthen ourselves so that our emotional outputs stay intact, as well as purposeful to our spiritual growth. God bless you!

Love, Red

Dear you,

Rise up and lead from the front! For today is the day for you to be set free from the brutality of turmoil and/or the chains restraining you. Don't let nothing hold you back, not even yourself. Jesus was sent here to free you from these brutal chains of life, to end your turmoil through His death. In fact John 8:36 says, "So if the Son sets you free, you will be free indeed!" True freedom begins at salvation and the power in the name of Jesus breaks your chains and overcomes the turmoil! Be easy today, be at peace and choose to be set free. God bless you!

Love, Red

Dear you,

Raise your expectations; don't limit yourself to simply be good, be great! Today is going to be your day to grow, to bounce back from adversity and to lead from the front with raised expectations! Oh yes, you will face those with doubt and/or those that want to see you fail, but that's okay…loving those that despise or hate you, grows you! I encourage each of us to live in a higher state of expectation, a state of forward progress, resting in the fact that greatness is our destiny! I leave you with 1 Peter 1:3–5 (MSG), "What a God we have! And how fortunate we are to have him, this Father of our Master Jesus! Because Jesus was raised from the dead, we've been given a brand-new life and have everything to live for, including a future in heaven—and the future starts now! God is keeping careful watch over us and the future. The Day is coming when you'll have it all—life healed and whole." God bless you!

Love, Red

DEAR YOU

Dear you,

Breakthrough is visual evidence of your "beenthrough." You see, we all hit those symbolic potholes (maybe addictions or finances), get flat tires (possibly depression, loss of loved ones), encounter engine malfunctions (maybe health problems), as well as experience the normal wear and tear (age). We each travel through our own beenthrough, which is evidenced in our breakthrough. Attempting to judge another's journey because their breakthrough doesn't replicate ours isn't right or justified. Jeff Eastham once said "Never judge another person's BREAKTHROUGH until you first understand their BEENTHROUGH!" In other words, like the message version of Matthew 7:1–5 in part says, "It's this whole traveling road-show mentality all over again, playing a holier-than-thou part instead of just living your part. Wipe that ugly sneer off your own face, and you might be fit to offer a washcloth to your neighbor." We are called to love, not to judge or hate. Legacies are created in part by how we overcome our beenthrough and live out our breakthrough.

Love, Red

Dear you,

Stress, if not managed and balanced, can produce behavior that causes people to berate others or become "that person" considered as unapproachable. Becoming unapproachable, or one known to berate others, is not suitable behavior, especially for a leader. If not put in check, eventually, stress will lead to relationship breakdowns, not to mention the wretched tale of those metaphorical burnt bridges. Don't be that person; THINK before you act, be wise, slow to speak, and don't forget the element of compassion…maybe you need to implore its presence. Allow James 1:19 to inspire your daily life, "Understand this, my dear brothers and sisters: You must all be quick to listen, slow to speak, and slow to get angry." Stay solid, compassionate, and approachable. God bless you!

Love, Red

Dear you,

The whole world is full of everybody else, so be yourself; recognize that each breath is a new chance to eliminate the "can'ts" in life, replacing them with the "cans" because you "can" and you will! Live life with purpose and live it well; after all, you are created in God's image (Genesis 1:27). Simply know that you CAN, and it's up to you to say, "I WILL!" God bless you.

Love, Red

DEAR YOU

Dear you,

Other people's actions tend to influence how you respond; however, the way you respond is still your choice. Don't let negative people impact your happiness found in your God walk. A wise Proverb found in 15:1 says, "A soft answer turneth away wrath: but grievous words stir up anger." The point? Don't give others the pleasure of bringing you down to their level; lift them up to yours.

Love, Red

Dear you,

The seemingly insignificant moments, those routine life interactions, can be more significant than you think. For in those insignificant moments, some of the most significant changes can happen within your life. Johann Wolfgang von Goethe once said, "There is nothing insignificant in the world. It all depends on the point of view." I encourage you to value the significance of the seemingly insignificant, because God has a purpose for all things; Jeremiah 29:11 and Romans 8:28 are great references and worthy to remember. Well, as you get after today, remember to value the power found within the seemingly insignificant interactions; they just might lead to a significant life changing moment. God bless you!

Love, Red

Dear you,

Take a breath, a big one. You feel that? That right there is called life, your freedom to live and time to make an impact on your legacy. No truer freedom exists than the freedom found in your Heavenly relationship. Don't let fear of failure or your past stop you from living today, for tomorrow is yet to come and yesterday is dead and gone. Take another deep breath and realize that fear of failure or doubts have no place in your life and their strongholds can only be broken by the Mighty King of Kings! Psalm 34:4 says, "I prayed to the Lord, and He answered me. He freed me from all my fears." Live life, live it well and die right. Have no fear and use your breath to love, reach and serve; leave a legacy to remember! God bless you!

Love, Red

Dear you,

You mustn't allow anxiety to have a foothold; for, anxiety feeds chaos and chaos, if not managed, slowly weakens and destroys. Charles Spurgeon once said, "Anxiety does not empty tomorrow of its sorrows, but only empties today of its strength." As a leader, manage the expectations, eliminate chaos and remain the constant example of wisdom; be the calming force among the chaos and anxious. I leave you with a prayer, found in Psalm 139:23–24, to assist in your life journey: "Search me, O God, and know my heart; test me and know my anxious thoughts. Point out anything in me that offends you, and lead me along the path of everlasting life." God bless you!

Love, Red

DEAR YOU

Dear you,

Be honest, follow through with what you say; for your actions speak louder than words. Reminds me of what William Shakespeare once said, "No legacy is so rich as honesty!" How is your legacy looking? Everything you do represents who you say you are. Can others count on you to stand by your word, to mean what you say and follow through with doing what you say? I leave you with Colossians 3:23 "Work willingly at whatever you do, as though you were working for the Lord rather than for people." Honesty and integrity go hand in hand; are they in yours? God bless you.

Love, Red

Dear you,

Bitterness weakens, forgiveness strengthens. Staying angry or bitter leads to an internal demolition derby; it leaves you as a self-inflicted victim of stolen peace, hurting, smashed up, and broken. "For every minute you remain angry, you give up sixty seconds of peace of mind" (Ralph Waldo Emerson). Remember, when you are in life's demolition derby, strive to lead from the front. Stay encouraged and set yourself free. I leave you with what Jesus said in Matthew 6:14–15, "If you forgive those who sin against you, your heavenly Father will forgive you. But if you refuse to forgive others, your Father will not forgive your sins." God bless you!

Love, Red

Dear you,

Keep the praise and prayer in your life on point. Praise God because He loves you! Pray to Him because He hears you! And rejoice in knowing that you serve a Mighty God with inseparable love for you! No matter what you are facing or going through He has you covered by the blood and wrapped in His arms of love! NOTHING…I repeat…NOTHING can you separate you from His love. Romans 8:38–39 confirms it! Now get up and get that soul churning with some mighty praise and prayer for and to a Mighty God. God bless you!

Love, Red

Dear you,

Don't give up on yourself, stay committed to becoming a stronger you; I believe in you! Commitment in making your core beliefs deeper, your core convictions stronger, and your core competencies expanded, simply put, is up to you. Your level of commitment, to those self-values, contributes to your overall team values; after all, the team consists of multiple players, many coming with different values but have sense enough to align their commitments by leaning forward for the betterment of the team. Vince Lombardi once said, "Individual commitment to a group effort—that is what makes a team work, a company work, a society work, a civilization work." I encourage you to stay solid in your self-commitment in consistently being a stronger and better you; for this directly impacts your team. Don't just think about it or hope for the best, live it and influence the rest. I like Peter Drucker's savvy spin on it, "Unless commitment is made, there are only promises and hopes…but no plans." Spiritually, success comes from committing all actions to Him; Proverbs 16:3 says, "Commit your actions to the Lord, and your plans will succeed." God bless you as you get after increasing your commitment!

Love, Red

Dear you,

With wisdom comes knowledge; with knowledge comes understanding. So with each decision you make, think about the short term, as well as the long term, effects. Only you can seek wisdom, only you can choose to expand your knowledge and only you can apply them both to understanding the decisions you choose to make. Just remember that when you seek God's wisdom your knowledge widens and your understanding deepens. Proverbs 2:10–11 says, "For wisdom will enter your heart, and knowledge will fill you with joy. Wise choices will watch over you. Understanding will keep you safe." Build a wise legacy, a legacy filled with Godly knowledge. God bless you!

Love, Red

Dear you,

Be self-aware, especially in what you speak. For what comes out of your mouth has the tendency to affect others, which is why it's so important to have your words packed with truth. Truth endures, lies fade away. I encourage you to stay truthful and at your best, as your legacy influences the rest. Proverbs 12:19 says, "Truthful lips endure forever, but a lying tongue is but for a moment." God bless you.

Love, Red

Dear you,

Love is as love does. "I love you"; these words in action show the worth of the words spoken. God's love empowers you to keep on keeping on while overcoming those lonely, life damaging, downward spirals, which is why you mustn't underestimate the power of love in action. After all, love is the greatest and 1 Corinthians 13 is packed full of what it is; I leave you verses 4–7 for you to apply. Just imagine what life could be like if we all lived by the following. "Love is patient and kind. Love is not jealous or boastful or proud or rude. It does not demand its own way. It is not irritable, and it keeps no record of being wronged. It does not rejoice about injustice but rejoices whenever the truth wins out. Love never gives up, never loses faith, is always hopeful, and endures through every circumstance." I love you and pray for your life to be God filled and fantastic!

Love, Red

Dear you,

Courage, a characteristic paired with strength, empowers you with confidence, as a solid leader, to lean forward, facing fear head on. Courage enables you to stay strong, pushing through some of the most broken and fearful times of your life. Believe it and stand tall, courageously face life and overcome the fear. Joshua 1:1–9 is a strong example of a Godly leadership journey, the journey of Joshua. Here you will discover the illustration of courage and strength required of a leader, as he led the people through fear with the reward of inheriting the lands that were promised to them. The core theme is that, through his leadership journey, God told him to be courageous, strong and faithful. The point? You and I have the same source of strength and courage at our disposal, if we simply seek it. I encourage you to lead from the front by staying strong and courageous, and never give up. God bless you!

Love, Red

DEAR YOU

Dear you,

Henry Cloud once said, "Everything has seasons, and we have to be able to recognize when something's time has passed and be able to move into the next season." Are you ready for a new season in your life? Perhaps, your current lifestyle is brewing a much needed change. It's okay; change is a part of life. People around you may not always understand or accept your choice of change, but at the end of the day it's about becoming a better and stronger you. So don't fear pruning the areas in your life needed in order to foster the required change. Ecclesiastes 3:1–8 is a solid reference. I leave you with verse 1 "For everything there is a season, and a time for every matter under heaven..." God bless you.

Love, Red

Dear you,

"Rejoice in the Lord always: and again I say, Rejoice" (Philippians 4:4). That's right, no matter what...REJOICE. Yes, there will be scary and rough times in life. Do not...I repeat...do not let circumstances change you for the worst. No matter what you're going through, whether it be health issues, family issues, work issues, etc., stand strong; realize that God knows you are strong enough to face whatever it is you are facing. Through the good and bad, you and I face in life, we have to hold steady and believe that we are strong enough to overcome. As the old saying goes, "The will of God will never take you where the grace of God will not protect you." Praying for you to have a super fantastic day. Stand ready, stand strong and rejoice! God bless you.

Love, Red

Dear you,

GET BACK UP and SHAKE IT OFF! Have you ever seen a person walking along and they hit that slick spot and start doing a little dance to keep their balance? I'm sure you have; it might have even been you. If they're lucky they catch themselves before the fall; however, many times they crash to the ground. Most of the time, God willing, they get back up and shake it off. This reminds me of life. Every once in a while we hit those slick spots, those slippery slopes causing us to do a little dance to stay balanced, and sometimes the slick or slope is so slippery we come crashing down. GET BACK UP, SHAKE IT OFF! I encourage you to consistently keep the fight for your life strong, GET BACK UP and SHAKE IT OFF; for God is the rock in your storms, the rock in your calm. As you negotiate the slicks and slopes of life, keep 1 Thessalonians 5:18 in your hip pocket God bless you!

Love, Red

DEAR YOU

Dear you,

Routine maintenance is done to prevent mechanical breakdowns. When you find something bad, you fix it. In other words, you do your best to identify and correct the root cause of failure to extend the life of the product. Applying this technique to your relationships and life is important. Why? Because it's relationships that impact your life and it's your legacy to maintain. If the root cause of failure is not identified and corrected, your relationships, life and legacy begin to slowly breakdown. I encourage you to conduct routine maintenance on your life and tighten up any loose ends to prevent those life breakdowns! The good news is that no one is beyond repair in the eyes of God; He loves you so much (Romans 5:8) and even set up a way (1 John 1:9) for you to stay maintained. Now, get after it today; I believe in you and know you will be the best life mechanic around and will have a fine-tuned legacy, one to remember! God bless you! Live life, live it well, and die right!

Love, Red

Dear you,

This weather is like life. The beautiful sunny days represent the happy and fantastic times in life, the rainy days represent daily struggles and the storms represent life's obstacles. It's a cycle dependent upon the climate in which you live, which is like life—a cycle. It's you who establishes the climate of life you choose, or better yet, allow. When the sun breaks back out it reminds me that no matter the rain or storms, if we hold on and keep on keeping on we will see the sun shine once again. The key is to persevere. This is why I choose to stand and never give up on this God life or you. Stay encouraged and keep that throttle of life twisted; pushing through life's storms. God bless you and may you experience God's love in ways you never have before.

Love, Red

Dear you,

Relationships are about being there for one another in numerous ways. So why do many relationships start off strong, but tend to fall apart? Human pride and lack of humble attitudes. We live in a selfish and prideful world full of people wanting to prove they are the greatest, even if they have to destroy others to reach the top, which is why it's important to remember that pride will eventually destroy you and your relationships. In fact, Proverbs 16:18 says, "Pride goes before destruction, and haughtiness before a fall." I encourage you to implement a little bit more humility and trust in your life; be willing to serve those around you in ways you never have, trusting that God has a plan for you. God bless you!

Love, Red

Dear you,

Stop living substandard; be bold and confident! Mature growth is evident when you recognize that sometimes, you need a transformation in your paradigm when it comes to your very own self-confidence! If your standards keep you down instead of building you up, then you need a self-revolution, a redefining of who you are and where you want to be! Set standards, uphold standards and believe you will exceed the standard. The standards you set for yourself trickle down to the standards and quality of your team. Ray Kroc said, "The quality of a leader is reflected in the standards they set for themselves." Remember, leadership starts with you! Spiritually, your confidence is found in Him. Second Corinthians 3:17 says, "For the Lord is the Spirit, and wherever the Spirit of the Lord is, there is freedom." Be bold, be confident and be free in all things. God bless you! I believe in you!

Love, Red

Dear you,

Haters gonna hate; influence them instead of them changing you! Don't let deficiencies in other's actions constitute negative reactions on your part; for those second and third order effects can bite you in the butt! You're a leader (even when you think you aren't, someone in your life is watching), which means your actions matter, your attitude drives, and your mannerisms are emulated. Yes, people can be ungrateful, downright mean, and/or self-serving; however, don't consider it a negative thing, rather look at it as an accountability thing directly allowing you to show just how well you live outwardly by faith. It's the way you handle the unnatural, and natural, pressures of life that directly shows others that you do indeed serve a mighty God. James 1:2–4 is great! I leave you with verse 3, "For you know that when your faith is tested, your endurance has a chance to grow." I believe in you and want to see you grow. God bless you.

Love, Red

Dear you,

When it comes to life, you show those around you exactly who you are, not by words, but through your actions! You're living, breathing and heart beating proof that Jesus is very much real and alive. From experience, walking out life's good and bad with faith is hard sometimes, but rewarding every time. Don't fear changing the areas that need changing; maintain a hell limiting, yet limitless, relationship with God! Keep your relationship with Jesus real and real actions will naturally follow. First John 1:9 will help you along the way. Praying for God to bless all aspects of your life!

Love, Red

Dear you,

Passion is vital in keeping your inner thrive and drive alive, especially if you expect your legacy to survive. Passion is the known emotion accountable for the beginning of your dreams, as well as what enables you to build and fulfill them. I encourage you to firmly race after your purpose, fulfill your dreams and leave a winner's legacy. Just keep in mind, spiritually, your passion to thrive to be more like God and keep the drive alive in fulfilling your God purpose is essential in your pursuit of that eternal prize. I leave you with 1 Corinthians 9:24–25, "Don't you realize that in a race everyone runs, but only one person gets the prize? So run to win! All athletes are disciplined in their training. They do it to win a prize that will fade away, but we do it for an eternal prize." Stay disciplined, stand up, stand out, and step to it; don't snuff out your passion! God bless you.

Love, Red

Dear you,

Many of us have worked on something greasy; leaving us dirty and unpresentable, yet not unacceptable. To clean up hard grease, dirt and/or grime you can use this product called "Fast Orange"; it has the power to leave you presentable and acceptable. This reminds me of life; many of us go through life getting dirty, unpresentable, yet not unacceptable. In fact, sometimes, we let our life build up to that nasty metaphorical stage of caked on grease. What do we do? We turn to the Bible, our Fast Orange, and get cleaned up. God sees us as acceptable and through Him we are made presentable. First John 1:9 says, "If we confess our sins, He is faithful and just to forgive us our sins and to cleanse us from all unrighteousness." Are you ready to be cleaned? God bless you!

Love, Red

DEAR YOU

Dear you,

A solid Proverb found in 4:23 says, "Guard your heart above all else, for it determines the course of your life." Some of your greatest creative accomplishments are first created in your mind by what lies within your heart of hearts; in other words, what's inside will not always be able to hide; for what's in your heart will eventually claw its way out. What will claw out of you? Are you on the right ride? I encourage you, as you allow your creative juices to flow, to keep that Proverb in your hip pocket, along with what the Psalmist said in Psalm 25:4–5, which says, "Show me the right path, O Lord; point out the road for me to follow. Lead me by your truth and teach me, for you are the God who saves me. All day long I put my hope in you." God bless you.

Love, Red

Dear you,

I was out on the front porch, taking in the calm after the storm. To the right was a beautiful sunset that reminded me of sitting on a beach taking in the pristine rays of light from heaven above. Can you imagine it, the beach, warmth and beautiful rays of light? To the immediate left was the darkness of clouds, which reminded me of the darkness of hell. As the darkness encroached upon the rays of light, the pristine rays pierced through the oncoming darkness, breaking through the symbolic darkness of hell. This reminded me of our life lived with the light of Christ. No matter the hell and darkness we encounter, the light of Christ is pristine and shines bright…piercing through our darkest moments of hell on earth. Led me to John 1; I leave you with verse 5: "The light shines in the darkness, and the darkness has not overcome it."

Love, Red

Dear you,

Life is like incoming rain. Before it rains, the wind picks up, delivering that tranquil smell of rain in the air. The clouds roll in, thunder rolls, lightning strikes and here comes the rain, providing the water needed for nature, God's way of washing away the grime. Once the rain passes, you have that distinct fresh smell, or sense, of clean consuming the very air you breathe and freshness in the nature around…that sense of peace. Reminds me of life, with challenges being symbolic to rain. Before the challenge hits, your spirit senses it; at least most of the time. These challenges are opportunities to be provided the drops of faith needed, the cleansing wisdom sought and the thunderous knowledge to overcome. Then, once the challenge is overcome, like the passing rain, you have a distinct sense of accomplishment, a new-found strength in faith, deepened wisdom and increased knowledge. So in essence, the challenges you face are pathways for you to be washed new, avenues to grow and solid opportunities to wipe away the grime in your life—all symbolic to growth. I encourage each of us to grow, endure and let the Holy Spirit flow. I believe in you and know you will succeed! Take the time to hit up Romans 5, as you endure and wipe away life's grime. God bless you!

Love, Red

Dear you,

Don't let the failures of the past dictate your present, nor let your present be overlooked by focusing simply on your future. Your here and now is your opportunity to define the future, rather than be confined by your past. So make the most of today, as you continue to build that solid legacy. Keep your revolution and revival alive.

Love, Red

Dear you,

Relationships require work and part of the work is up to you; it's aligning and maximizing core capabilities that each one brings to the table. Keep in mind that relationships are growing, living, ever changing and constantly evolving. So be diligent in your endeavors and open your eyes to the BIG picture, recognizing the second and third order effects of your actions, for it is those actions that either strengthen or weaken your relationships. I encourage you to set aside any root of a self-serving attitude and be more selfless. It's not hard, keep it simple; apply Luke 6:31, "Do to others as you would like them to do to you." God bless you!

Love, Red

Dear you,

Life is like a tree; your life represents a leaf on that tree. Seasons change and the leaves fade away, but the cool part is that, when the new season arrives, new life buds from the tree. The point? I encourage you to nurture your life tree and prune the bad leaves off so that new growth in your life blossoms. Proverbs 27:1 says, "Don't brag about tomorrow, since you don't know what the day will bring." Be ready today to meet Jesus face to face…for this could be your last day; if tomorrow comes count it as a blessing and be a blessing as you grow in Him. Well, as you get after it today, fertilize your life tree with Mark 12:30 and allow Him to prepare you for your next season. Will you let him? God bless you.

Love, Red

Dear you,

Building relationships require commitment, along with a deep burning passion to keep them alive. Solid ones are made up of selfless versus selfish acts. Henry Ford said, "Coming together is a beginning; keeping together is a progress; working together is success." So as you self-examine your existing relationships ask yourself, "Am I upholding my part of the commitment and working together to succeed?" Make progress together and remember what Winston Churchill said, "Success is not final, failure is not fatal: it is the courage to continue that counts." God bless you today.

Love, Red

Dear you,

As I sit here, drinking a cup of coffee, I'm reminded how thankful I am for the little things, such as a cup and electricity; for without these two things it makes drinking coffee doable, but a bit difficult. I encourage you to take time to notice the little things in your life, taking note on how they impact the big. Spiritually, be thankful for the little things, such as a verse or prayer. For without these two things life is doable, but with them your God life stays on point. Simply, cherish all things good in your life and, as Psalm 136 says, "Give thanks to the God of heaven. His faithful love endures forever." That's right, His love endures forever! Well, I'm praying for you to have a safe and great week! God bless you!

Love, Red

Dear you,

Stay rich in attitude and character, because it doesn't matter how much, or little, you have if your character and attitude are bankrupt. Keep in mind that a bankrupt character and attitude can only be disguised for so long before the truth is exposed. The point is that it doesn't matter how clean someone is on the outside if they are dirty on the inside; they still dirty. The balance of your internal wheel influences how effectively you spin your external wheel. Spiritually, your attitude and character should be Christ driven, rich with the fruits of the Spirit as found in Galatians 5:22–23, "love, joy, peace, patience, kindness, goodness, faithfulness, gentleness, and self-control…" I encourage you to strive and thrive to increase your wealth in character and attitude by consistently working to be balanced and clean; be rich in both attitude and character. God bless you!

Love, Red

Dear you,

A life lived victorious starts with believing you are a victor! I encourage you to rise to life's circumstances by generating a self-disposition fueled with a victorious personality; allow it to resonate within your inner most core! I believe in you, don't give in to the circumstance, but rather endure the fight and be victorious! Winston Churchill once said, "Victory at all costs, victory in spite of all terror, victory however long and hard the road may be; for without victory, there is no survival." The point? God has enabled you to be victorious; Psalm 108:13 confirms it: "Through God we shall do valiantly: for He it is that shall tread down our enemies." So be a VICTOR, knowing that you are not alone, for God is with you! Survival requires believing that you are a conqueror and victor. Believe it! God bless you today!

Love, Red

Dear you,

Reputation is lifelong, forever ingrained into your legacy. Is yours worthy to remember or emulate? I encourage you to permanently carve loyalty and kindness into your heart; for they are two characteristics that deeply define your legacy. Their presence will be evident and reflected in your attitude and your will to never give up on yourself or others. Proverbs 3:3–4 says, "Never let loyalty and kindness leave you! Tie them around your neck as a reminder. Write them deep within your heart. Then you will find favor with both God and people, and you will earn a good reputation." Allow your legacy to spark a victorious revival in others; a spiritual revolution in your life and legacy is sure to show another the way. Live life, live it well, and die right. God bless you!

Love, Red

Dear you,

Johnny Cash, a staple in music history…a legend, was a self-professed believer as well as a guy that saw many dark and lonely spots in life. In fact, he wrote and sung many spiritually themed songs, realizing he needed the help of God; the thought of him going on without Him was no longer an option. He knew that believing in God doesn't make you weak, a self-righteous person or a person filled with false hope; it does, however, make you a stronger person, because you choose to believe and trust in someone you can't see. Just like Cash and me, don't let self-righteous Christ followers stop you from believing and accepting the only one that can give you Eternal Life, the one named Jesus. Ever since I gave the yesterdays gone wrong to God, my todays are so much richer. You, like Cash and me, will overcome through your strength in God. Just know that there's nothing weak about being meek or living for God week to week. Hit up Romans 10:9–10 God bless you.

Love, Red

Dear you,

Maximize your creativity, which is kept ablaze by bringing your imagination to life. Don't let fear or complacency prevent you from altering your reality, for life and death are simply a blink away; within each blink use your imagination to maximize your creation. I encourage you to never give up on what God has created in you! After all as one of His followers, He has made you new. Second Corinthians 5:17 says, "Therefore, if anyone is in Christ, the new creation has come: The old has gone, the new is here!" God bless you! Live life, live it well and die right.

Love, Red

Dear you,

Why limit your possibilities, when life is limitless? If you keep thinking about the chance but never take the chance you lose out on the chance, and that chance could just be the game-changing chance you need. Don't settle in life to just exist, be remarkable! Have the courage to stand up, stand out and stand firm in your quest of building a strong legacy, a legacy constructed on a solid foundation. First Corinthians 16:13–14 says, "Be on guard. Stand firm in the faith. Be courageous. Be strong. And do everything with love." I encourage you to never limit your best, as you influence the rest, and may you take the time to notice the little things, noting how they impact the big. Your legacy is at stake; get after the limitless possibilities! I believe in you! God bless you!

Love, Red

Dear you,

Bitterness gets you nowhere, but down into a deep dark place. It destroys you from the inside out; symbolically, clawing its way out the stronger and deeper you allow it to get. Yes, people and circumstances will make you angry, but letting that anger grow into wrath only destroys you, not the one you are angry with. Terry Brooks once said, "Hurt leads to bitterness, bitterness to anger, travel too far that road and the way is lost." You see, wrath is a seed that starts the growth of the root, which in turn will grow into full blown bitterness if not exterminated from your life. I encourage you to stay the course of positive, legacy creating, actions; remember, that grateful people are not bitter and bitter people are not grateful. I leave you with Hebrews 12:15, "Look after each other so that none of you fails to receive the grace of God. Watch out that no poisonous root of bitterness grows up to trouble you, corrupting many." God bless you!

Love, Red

Dear you,

Rise from the ashes of defeat! Rise up and get out of that metaphorical grave of living a substandard life. You are a somebody! Many times people tend to hold on tightly to what is loosely defined and loosely hold on to core values that are required to foster the change needed. It's up to you to set your standards high, to get back to key core values; once the wheels are set in motion, hold on tightly as you rise from the depths of defeat. I encourage you to take ownership and rise stronger than before; your rise might just be the spark needed to spark the motion of that positive synergy…ultimately producing results in your life that matter. In Ezekiel 37, God commanded a mass grave, known as the valley of dry bones, to rise from the ashes, putting them back together bone by bone, piece by piece, full of breath. The point? God can and will give you what you need in order to rise from the ashes of defeat! God bless you!

Love, Red

Dear you,

Do NOT let despair or hopelessness fuel your ride of life. You gotta change your outlook; view your ride of life half full vs. half empty. Focus on the positives you have and stop letting the negatives take the positives for granted. Positive mental change begins with you, YES you…it takes endurance…the will to never give up. Spiritually, concentrate on your Christ identity and you will find that your life tank is full knowing that, whatever life throws at you, HE has a purpose. Romans 5:1–5 is awesome motivation! Verse 5 says, "And this hope will not lead to disappointment. For we know how dearly God loves us, because he has given us the Holy Spirit to fill our hearts with his love." Christ's unconditional love for you and me…it never runs dry. God bless you!

Love, Red

Dear you,

We pray for peace, but stay prepared for war. Many aspects of freedom, life, families, and people are spiraling out of control. Lies are being spun into false truths. Lives are being taken. Children being set forth with no direction. Men not being the father or man they should be. Families destroying left and right. You catch the drift right? The very core values that founded this life are being stripped away, so transparent that nothing is left but memories of what was. Stand up, YOU are NOT alone! I leave you with it simply put, your word is your word; let it stand for truth, let it speak encouragement and let it build up, rather than tear down. As a follower of Christ, you are sanctified through Him, set apart for the Lord and consecrated for His uses and purposes. Let Him, an Almighty God, use you in mighty ways. In John 17:17 Jesus said in red letter, "Sanctify them by Your truth. Your Word is truth. As You sent Me into the world, I also have sent them into the world." Be prepared…be truth…and stand ready.

Love, Red

Dear you,

Today is your day; claim it! Go ahead and shout it. What are you waiting for? Shout it, "Today is my day!" Through life we all plant seeds. Maybe it's a dream, a business, career, a Word from God. Those seeds you've planted in your life are growing and require endurance on your part. Keep steady and remain true to nurturing whatever it is you planted. Your actions bring life to your seeds and yield results; without actions you can't expect reactions. Spiritually, you must endure through, strong in your faith, even when you face troubles. No pain, no gain. James 1:2–3 says, "Dear brothers and sisters, when troubles of any kind come your way, consider it an opportunity for great joy. For you know that when your faith is tested, your endurance has a chance to grow." Endure, be results-driven and seize each and every opportunity! God bless you.

Love, Red

Dear you,

Climb that mountain! With each step, dig in deeper, push yourself to go farther, believe in yourself, and don't stop until you reach the top; you can overcome! When you feel like you just can't climb no more, be reminded of the God that carries you, the God that said in Matthew 17:20b, "I tell you the truth, if you had faith even as small as a mustard seed, you could say to this mountain, 'Move from here to there,' and it would move. Nothing would be impossible!" I encourage you, as you steadily get after overcoming the mountainous obstacles of life, to look beyond the base of the mountain, see beyond the top of the mountain and see what lies in wait for you! You must believe in yourself if you want to experience the revolution and revival destined for your life! Praying for you and for your faith to be strengthened so that you know that, no matter what, nothing is impossible! God bless you!

Love, Red

Dear you,

Life requires courage; courage to do the right things for the right reasons, courage to give and receive correction, courage to use your voice for change, courage to stand back up when life knocks you down, courage to stand for your beliefs, the list can go on and on… The point is that courage is a key characteristic in being a strong, resilient and solid you. I encourage you to find the courage to never give up on the victorious revival and revolution possible in your life; keep onward with courage and never abandon in love. I leave you with 1 Corinthians 16:13–14, "Be on guard. Stand firm in the faith. Be courageous. Be strong. And do everything with love." God bless you!

Love, Red

Dear you,

Your mind can be your worse prison; however, the prison of the mind is a prison built with penetrable walls. That's right, penetrable! It's a new day, a day filled with new opportunities to rise up out of your self-built prison. Your legacy is yours to create and it doesn't have to be defined or confined by metaphorical walls. You have the power in you to be great! So get up, get ready, and get started on making things happen; focus on positive revolution and revival of your dreams and teams! I encourage you to demolish the walls, negotiate the obstacles and trust in God; allow Him to open your eyes to what He has already set in place for you. ACCOMPLISH GREATNESS…BE A LEADER! I leave you with a solid reference found in Psalm 16:1, "Preserve me, O God: for in thee do I put my trust." God bless you.

Love, Red

Dear you,

Raised expectations, for God to show up and show out in our life, are required for success. If we stay stuck in a first season mentality or a comfort season we miss out on the God Supply. We can't rely solely on the things of the past or present that work to push us forward to the future, we must use creativity and ingenuity to spark a new fire of growth that will draw others in; like bugs drawn to a light. We must believe in the promised harvest, but the corn or cotton doesn't pick itself; we have to dig deeper, open the doors to positive change. Change is inevitable. Now, God and his saving message has been, is and will stay the same, but the way to share His message must be in a constant state of positive movement…the rotation must continue. When a wheel stops moving, the vehicle stops and goes nowhere, but with continued rotation the vehicle continues to make progress. The key is in the direction of rotation; if we want forward progress to be reached, as well as continuous, we, must continue to move forward with change that positively affects our life. Let's light the fire of ingenuity, the fire of change and bring about a life changing, as well as spiritual, growth like never experienced.

Love, Red

DEAR YOU

Dear you,

Uplift, encourage, and inspire others along the way. You have the power to change your approach, your alliances, your routines, your attitude, your life; it's up to you. I will tell you that if you begin to make an effort then, yes, you might just spark a domino effect of genuine change within your circle, as well as those you encounter along the way. Your change might just be the example someone will model after. Perhaps, your change could also lead you in building solid alliances and partnerships. Well, I encourage you to stand strong, lead with integrity and exercise the strength and courage in being the change you know is needed within your life and circles; as a leader, lead from the front. I leave you with Hebrews 10:24, "Let us think of ways to motivate one another to acts of love and good works!" God bless you!

Love, Red

Dear you,

Stop being your worst enemy, stop giving up on yourself and eliminate fear—crawl, walk, run. Represent the ideas you have, bring them to life! Yes, many wait to see if you will fail or fall below some man-made standards. In fact, there are some just waiting for the opportunity to show you how you have or will fail. Shut them down; show those that want to pit you against failure that you won't' fall trap to it, that you stand firm in God's promises! You are not permanently where you are meant to be; BELIEVE IT…RECEIVE IT! The hits will come and knock you down, GET UP; pick yourself up and walk through the pains of growth! Let nothing…I repeat… nothing stand in your way! I pray for you, as Paul prayed in Romans 15:13. God bless you!

Love, Red

Dear you,

Use wisdom in your decisions; live wisely and stay positively well. Put negativity behind you, at least do your part to minimize your today and future from it. Why? Because your happiness starts with you. You alone are responsible for your decisions. Live today and this year with purpose. We each must step up and take charge of our lives and hold ourselves accountable before attempting to rightfully be there for our brothers, sisters, and family. "WE" is comprised of you…so make you the best so that you influence the rest. I encourage you to pray, as David did in Psalm 90:15 "Give us gladness in proportion to our former misery! Replace the evil years with good." God bless you!

Love, Red

Dear you,

Welcome to the first day of the rest of your life! Don't look back to the past, that midnight smoke, tokes, or the whiskey and cokes; look forward and set in motion solid improvement in the areas needed within your life. As the cliche goes, "Out with the old and in with the new." Let this year be the year for you to value forward progress, as well as a year for you to teach your up and coming its value. Live this life full of honor and integrity, the year is yours to define who and what you are. Let your life lead by example and build a legacy that matters; one centered around being selfless versus selfish. Spiritually, give your life to God and become new in Him (2 Corinthians 5:17). Let Him fight your battles (Exodus 14:14) and always keep your trust in Him (Psalm 16:1). Bottom line is that none of us can undo last year, but we sure can make this one super fantastic year where we all make a difference while building solid legacies. Live life, live it well, love often, and die right. See you soon! God bless you!

Love, Red

DEAR YOU

Dear you,

End the year that's drawing near with positive focus, rather than an empty negative stare that leads you nowhere! I encourage you to enjoy your day, pray for those in need, never give up hope, lend a helping hand or listening ear, and, as always, cherish each second of each minute for your time on earth is drawing near. Stay strong as time carries on, for your road and journey has been long. You can do it; yes, you can, for the balance of the pendulum of time is in your hand. God bless!

Love, Red

Dear you,

From the heart: The year is almost over; if time continues for a couple more days, you can successfully say, "I MADE IT, I successfully overcame the year's ups and downs, sadness and joy, life and death. I AM AN OVERCOMER!" Each day is a sign of completing yesterday, followed with opportunities to live today. You see, life is short, we are but a mere breath away from death, but do not fear, for you are an OVERCOMER! Be reminded and encouraged of the sadness of Christ's death, turned to joy in His resurrection; for it's an instant reminder that, through Him, you are an OVERCOMER. John 16:33 says, "I have told you all this so that you may have peace in me. Here on earth you will have many trials and sorrows. But take heart, because I have overcome the world." So end the year with joy and bring in the new as a strong OVERCOMER! God bless you.

Love, Red

Dear you,

Commit to grow, commit to change, and learn to stay at your best in order to influence the rest! Change is inevitable; it's what you do with the change that affects your future. I encourage you to allow God to influence your change and back your commitments; for with Him you are bound to succeed. I leave you with a solid Proverb found in 16:3, "Commit your actions to the Lord, and your plans will succeed."

Love you, Red

Dear you,

If you're tired or worn out from life stresses quit holding on to them; lay them at Christ's feet, He lightens your load, and don't pick them back up. Allow God to fulfill His promises in your life. I leave you with a selection of Matthew 11:28–30 from the MSG version, "Are you tired? Worn out?... Come to me. Get away with me and you'll recover your life. I'll show you how to take a real rest...I won't lay anything heavy or ill-fitting on you. Keep company with me and you'll learn to live freely and lightly." So stay encouraged to let God give you the rest you seek. Well, God bless you and may you show someone the way...the lighter way of His way, TODAY.

Love you, Red

Dear you,

Passionate people tend to have their passion mistaken for a temper. Why? Because being passionate makes them passionate when what they are passionate about is threatened.

Love, Red

DEAR YOU

Dear you,

Don't let the bustle and hustle of the season rob you of the joy found in your Holy Ghost shuffle! God has enabled you to rejoice in all things! Remember, there is always someone worse off than you; count your blessings found within your shuffle and remember the people in need. Proverbs 21:13 says, "Those who shut their ears to the cries of the poor will be ignored in their own time of need." So stay strong and encouraged to increase the bustle in your Holy Ghost shuffle and to lend a helping hand to those in need. God bless you and know I love you.

Love, Red

Dear you,

Stay encouraged to influence the momentum of your life's pendulum, for the essence of time is priceless. Remember, just like a clock must stay balanced for the pendulum to properly sway, your life must continue to move in balance each and every day. For in the blink of an eye, your life could change forever; be careful what you do within the blink; cherish life by making forever memories.

Love, Red

Dear you,

Are you having doubts of God's relevance in your life and/or today's society? I know that sometimes we all face discouraging moments, leaving us with asking, "Where are You, Lord? Why are things the way they are?" Well, read the book of Proverbs; the book of Proverbs applies today just as it did years ago. You will see how alive God was then and is now! I read chapter 23, on to 24, this morning and then related it to today's world…the relevance jumped off the pages. So I encourage you to take the journey through Proverbs and allow Gods relevance in your life's journey to jump off the pages of His precious Word; you will hear Him speaking life-changing revelations on your today's perspectives; He will answer your questions. God bless you.

Love, Red

Dear you,

You have free will; use it to exercise love, discernment and wisdom in your actions, rather than in a disparaging and/or destructive way. Your here and now affects your tomorrow; for your actions today lay the foundation for how you'll cement your legacy. "I pray that your love will overflow more and more, and that you will keep on growing in knowledge and understanding. For I want you to understand what really matters, so that you may live pure and blameless lives until the day of Christ's return" (Philippians 1:9–10). God bless you.

Love you, Red

DEAR YOU

Dear you,

Multipurpose tools are handy. However, without your action it doesn't do what it was built to do; it sits idle until you put it to use. This reminds me of life; you have many tools at your disposable, both internal and external. However, without your action the tools in your life do you no good; just like the multi-purpose tool, they sit idle until put to use. Spiritually, the Bible is your solid tool for spiritual life work, but if it's never opened, used or applied it does no good, it simply collects dust like an old set of rusty tools. Mentally, perseverance is a great internal tool that leads to greatness. However, without your action greatness will not be achieved; for it takes the use of your tools. So in your quest for a better and stronger you, never underestimate the beauty and power of the surrounding tools available in your life for you to use. It's up to you to build up and/or repair your life journey; build a forever legacy. God bless you!

Love you, Red

Dear you,

Life is a journey of tears and laughter. When born, you get slapped in the butt to make you cry, pain and tears are seen in birth, followed by laughter and many joys along the way. Throughout our dash of life we all have life moments consisting of both, tears and laughter. Then, one day, we all will die and the tears begin to flow again, followed by laughter from loved ones as they reminisce on the fond memories shared. My encouragement to you, since life is filled with tears and laughter, to welcome the tears, but let laughter prevail. Live life, live it well, and die right. God bless you!

Dear you,

You can't find happiness in tomorrow; it's yet to come and you don't know what will be. However, happiness can be found in this very moment; for in this moment you have life. Don't let life pass by with empty memories. The air you breathe in will take place; it's what you do with the breath, while creating your legacy that enables you to find the perfect place to be ever present in the future of memories brought to life. Live life as if today is your last. God bless you!

Love, Red

Dear you,

People look up to you, to include your attributes. They want to see if you act on your duty to loyalty; yes, people do look at your level of determination to fulfill your duty in life as an example. Respect for yourself allows you to respect others, as well as the process of life. A life lived selfless exhibits integrity; a selfless life to emulate, along with great attributes, is Jesus. Be a leader, not an empty follower.

Love, Red

Dear you,

A pedestal—the imaginary platform where pride will knock you down. A lot of people tend to put themselves up on pedestals, don't be that person; they let material things and life status define them. Now, nothing wrong with being successful, but how you let that affect who you are will be noticed. A humble person reaps far more rewards and success in life than one driven by pride. Evaluate yourself; are you letting pride knock you down, rather than allowing God's wisdom to build you up? It's up to you to be defined as humble, known for your wisdom. Proverbs 11:2 says, "Pride leads to disgrace, but with humility comes wisdom." So as Tim McGraw sang, "Always stay humble and kind…don't take for granted the love this life gives you…and help the next one in line." God bless you!

Love, Red

Dear you,

Many times, after diligent preparation, we start the day with the intent to fulfill our life plans and/or goals. However, the reality is that plans and/or goals may change, are foiled, or are never meant to have been; but if it's part of God's plan in your life nothing will stand in the way. Ultimately, if you diligently seek Him, you will fulfill the plan, the plan He has for you. Proverbs 21:30 says, "No human wisdom or understanding or plan can stand against the Lord." So don't be discouraged if your plans change; stay encouraged even when you don't understand the "why" found within the change, for Proverbs 20:24 says, "The Lord directs our steps, so why try to understand everything along the way?" God bless you, as you fulfill His plans for your life. Now get up and after those goals!

Love, Red

Dear you,

Natural instincts prepare you for the change of seasons, instinctively, setting the course for new. Seasons change in our lives, which is why you should prepare on a daily basis for the storms, the shifts in climates and follow through with change by exhibiting the wisdom to be prepared. Wisdom and knowledge saves lives, make them part of your natural instincts. Proverbs 24:5 says, "The wise are mightier than the strong, and those with knowledge grow stronger and stronger." I encourage you to pay attention to nature, for you can learn a lot, and sharpen your natural instincts. God bless you!

Love, Red

Dear you,

Natural instincts prepare you for the change of life seasons, instinctively, setting the course for greatness! Greatness is achieved through actions not words, and you'll never achieve greatness if you never try. In your quest for greatness never underestimate the magnificence and power of serving another; a sure sign of greatness is recognized by consistently putting others before yourself. Spiritually, it's a no brainer. We are to reflect the Son of God, who was the ultimate in greatness, and solid example of servanthood. Matthew 20:28 says, "For even the Son of Man came not to be served but to serve others and to give His life as a ransom for many." Praying for you and may God bless you. Believe in yourself.

Love, Red

DEAR YOU

Dear you,

Sitting on the bank of a river clears and/or calms your mind. However, if you only focus on the other side of the river you miss out on the peace and tranquility that comes from experiencing, and listening to, the movement of the water. Reminds me of life and the problems we face; if we only focus on the problems we miss out on the peace and tranquility found in the great things that are passing by right in front of our eyes. Yes, you will experience moments where you fill overwhelmed, stressed and/or beaten down; this is when you allow John 16:33 to resonate inside your soul "I have told you all this so that you may have peace in Me. Here on earth you will have many trials and sorrows. But take heart, because I have overcome the world." I encourage you to balance life's problems, as you get to the other side of the river; just don't let great things pass you by. You are an OVERCOMER! God bless you.

Love, Red

Dear you,

It's not all about you; it's about your team and the folks you encounter along the way. Solid team players don't give up on one another, but rather depend on one another. Through your ride of life, show the power of looking forward, not back at mistakes. Learn from your mistakes, but don't focus on them. Lead the way in example for your team, by picking up where you failed yesterday and succeed today. In the words of Sonny Barger, "When you are a member of an organization, life isn't only about you. As part of a circle of people who depend on one another, you watch one another's back and remain loyal. I always look ahead, to the side, but never back." Be encouraged to make progress, look forward not backward; and, as it says in Ephesians 4:31–32, "Get rid of all bitterness, rage, anger, harsh words, and slander, as well as all types of evil behavior. Instead, be kind to each other, tenderhearted, forgiving one another, just as God through Christ has forgiven you." God bless you!

Love, Red

Dear you,

It's never too late to achieve something new; fundamentally, you must replace negativity with positivity, that "can do" approach. In fact Willie Nelson once said, "Once you replace negative thoughts with positive ones, you'll start having positive results." I encourage you to have the courage in stepping out and up into something new and positive. Don't fear the unknown, imagine the possibilities! I leave you with Matthew 7:7, "Keep on asking, and you will receive what you ask for. Keep on seeking, and you will find. Keep on knocking, and the door will be opened to you." God bless you.

Love, Red

Dear you,

Your life mustn't be just about what you get, but also about what you give. Material things pass away when you die, but your legacy lives on. Will your legacy be one to remember? Can you say you invested in people rather than soulless things? There are people in your life that need you, look up to you, as well as watch your pursuit of life. "Store your treasures in heaven, where moths and rust cannot destroy, and thieves do not break in and steal. Wherever your treasure is, there the desires of your heart will also be" (Matthew 6:20–21). In the words of Winston Churchill, "We make a living by what we get, but we make a LIFE by what we give." Pursue life, but don't forget those you can help along the way and leave a legacy to emulate. God bless you!

Love, Red

Dear you,

Being humble and meek doesn't translate to being weak. Being humble, meek, and the first to show kindness, shows mature wisdom. Proverbs 24:5–6 says, "The wise are mightier than the strong, and those with knowledge grow stronger and stronger." So don't show up to life's battles without wise guidance obtained from the Lord; victory depends on Godly wisdom. I pray for you today and for God's favor to shine upon you and yours; allow your eyes to be opened to the strength of wisdom, to include the ability to be meek, humble and the first to extend the olive branch. The strength of one is better than none. God bless you. I love you and know that the best is yet to come.

Love, Red

Dear you,

Think of your ride of life in terms of music; for music is an expression of emotions. You have sharp moments, flat moments, melodies, moments of harmony, highs and lows and much more; the correlation could go on and on. Like life right? Some classical, some contemporary, some thrash, a little hip-hop, some country, etc. The song style and lyric is yours to write. I encourage you to turn your life into a masterpiece, one that has the legacy to stay on the charts of life. Just be careful to appreciate and enjoy even the shortest note, for life is short. If you have writers block, just remember that God will help compose your life song, He delivers redemption. Zephaniah 3:17b says, "He will rejoice over you with joyful songs." God bless.

Love, Red

Dear you,

Sometimes it feels like life has punched you in the face, while standing toe to toe with life's adversity and trials. But wait…you also have moments of victory, defeating those trials. YES! It's through your testimony of overcoming that speaks louder than words! Yes, you have hurts, but you also receive healing from God. Yes, you will face disappointments, but you also have those divine appointments of victory! When you look to God's unconditional love and mercy you will realize that, through His unending power, those worries, hurts, disappointments, and insecurities fade away and are turned into moments of unquestionable divine delivery. God wants good, not bad, for you. He says in Jeremiah 29:11, "For I know the plans I have for you," says the Lord. "They are plans for good and not for disaster, to give you a future and a hope." So yes, there is always divine confidence and hope, as you stand toe to toe with life's adversity and trials. Be blessed and share a blessing. God bless you.

Love, Red

Dear you,

Appreciate the gift of life! Today, open your eyes and see the implementation of your vision, which is directly evidenced through the fruition of your mission! You mustn't let the mistakes of yesterday, nor the uncertainty of tomorrow, stop you from living life, for Him, today! Our earthly time will pass, it's our spiritual life that lasts; hence the importance of knowing that God, as one of His children, has great things in store for you. First Corinthians 2 is a great message of Wisdom, written to us by Paul, as He was inspired by God. Verse 9 says, "No eye has seen, no ear has heard, and no mind has imagined what God has prepared for those who love Him." I encourage you to seek His wisdom, modeling yours after His, and open your eyes to life's possibilities. For it's through His wisdom, where He will reveal what you cannot see with earthly eyes. God bless you!

Love, Red

DEAR YOU

Dear you,

Look at the world and you will see chaos and fear, along with seeing the safety found in happiness and order, which takes courage. Mainstream wants you to focus on the chaos and fear so that you will stay in a state of unrest. I encourage you to have the courage to change how you look at life; seek out the good, become the happy, establish self-order and dominate the fear. Mark Twain said, "Courage is resistance to fear, mastery of fear, not absence of fear." Spiritually, you do not stand alone. Joshua 1:9 reads, "This is my command—be strong and courageous! Do not be afraid or discouraged. For the Lord your God is with you wherever you go." Up to you to stand united. You have the power through God to eliminate and dominate the chaos. God bless you.

Love, Red

Dear you,

You have to deal with life, both the good and bad, those monsters we all face from time to time; there's really no running away. Sometimes these monsters lead to explosive events; be diligent in attempting to never be the reason for explosive situations, but be sure to stand for what's right and be the solution. Solid solutions come from self-respect, which comes before earning respect. The point is that self-respect requires self-discipline. Georges Braque said, "Truth exists; only lies are invented." What's in your soul finds its way out; the truth doesn't hide for long, it eventually comes to light. I encourage you to hit up two of my life verses to help you, as you keep rolling up on the good and eliminating the monsters, Psalm 16:1 and Exodus 14:14. God bless you!

Love, Red

Dear you,

You're only as good as you will be today. Do you hear what I'm saying? Yesterday is gone and tomorrow may not come. LIVE and LOVE today like it's ONCE in a lifetime opportunity, because it is! Love is deeper than how often it's tossed around in this life. First Corinthians 13:4–7 is spot on…read it. Verse 7 reads, "Love never gives up, never loses faith, is always hopeful, and endures through every circumstance." Be the one that puts real meaning back into the word "LOVE" and show your Brother or Sister the way! God bless you!

Love, Red

Dear you,

Ingenuity sparks a vision; the vision generates the mission; and the mission is measured in terms of goals. The lane of life you ride requires wisdom to effectively lean forward, arriving at the destination of implementing your ingenuity. Without wisdom, you'll have a rigid chapter in avoiding life's head-on collisions. Its wisdom that shows the way, paves the way and in fact creates a way; hence, the importance for you to search out wisdom in making your life lane a solid path full of successful ingenuity. Proverbs 28:26 says, "Those who trust their own insight are foolish, but anyone who walks in wisdom is safe." Stay encouraged and finish your ride of life with a legacy notable to remember. You can do it, even if you must pave the way! God bless you!

Love, Red

DEAR YOU

Dear you,

Throughout life you will encounter dark moments from time to time. I encourage you to remember that even in the darkest depths, a simple spark illuminates the way. Be the light and feed your spark, as you overcome these darkness laden situations; yes, you can do it! Pop your collar and stand tall, even in the darkest of hours; for the light of your spark will never fade when you continue to head the right way. Steadily get after the light, the light of Christ. Luke 1:78–79 says, "Because of God's tender mercy, the morning light from heaven is about to break upon us, to give light to those who sit in darkness and in the shadow of death, and to guide us to the path of peace." Follow His light, find peace. God bless you!

Love, Red

Dear you,

The people in your life matter; value and show appreciation for them. You can do it! The holidays shouldn't be the only time, or reason, you thank others, or the only time you show some love. With each heartbeat, be thankful and be one that is true through and through. Be inspired by the Apostle Paul, his writings in the book of Philemon are truly awe inspiring, especially during one of his times in jail. Even in jail he prayed for his family and friends and expressed his love and thanks for them. Oh, how great our world would be if we all exemplified Paul's thankfulness and prayers for his family and friends, despite being the one behind bars. Well, just as Paul, I thank God when I pray for you and appreciate having you in my life. I love you and I encourage you to join me in being forever thankful. Will you? God bless you!

Love, Red

Dear you,

Questioning circumstances won't change the circumstance; it's how you rise to the circumstance that defines your stance! Nowhere was it ever suggested that life would be easy, or circumstances avoided. However, your integrity and internal drive of the Holy Spirit directly enables you to have the ability to bear, as well as overcome, the circumstance. First Thessalonians 5:16–18, a powerful passage containing key actions to empower your legacy of being an overcomer, says, "Always be joyful. Never stop praying. Be thankful in all circumstances, for this is God's will for you who belong to Christ Jesus." I encourage you to rise to life's circumstances; generate a self-disposition fueled with a victorious personality, allow it to resonate within your inner most core, as you seek the power of the Holy Spirit in your ride of life! I believe in you, don't give in to the circumstance, but rather endure the fight and be victorious! God bless you today!

Love you, Red

Dear you,

May your heart give thanks; your belly stays full and may the love of your family grow deeper with each passing day! Don't let yesterday be the only time you give thanks and celebrate life. Colossians 3:17 says, "And whatever you do, in word or deed, do everything in the name of the Lord Jesus, giving thanks to God the Father through Him." I encourage you to give thanks in even the smallest things, for that is where some of the biggest blessings reside. Well, me and my family are praying for your day to be one of your best days yet! God bless you!

Love, Red

DEAR YOU

Dear you,

A powerful moment is when you realize the reality of your dreams and that you have the power to give them life! Dreams may just seem like dreams, but remember successful people, people like you and me, brought their dreams to life. I encourage you to eliminate boundaries that hold you back, believe in yourself and bring life to your dreams! I believe in you and know that you can be more than content, you can be overflowing with happiness and success. So don't let mediocrity hold you back from being exceptionally fabulous! God bless you!

Love, Red

Dear you,

To reap a harvest, you must plant the seed; the biggest harvest starts with some of the smallest seed! You see, there are many people hurting and in need of a God sent seed; the smallest word, act of kindness or simple phone call are all a type of this seed. The key is for each of us to do our part in planting the seeds; after all, we each are a planter and harvester of some sort. So whatever your gift is, please use it and show others the life changing power of Christ; steadily plant the seeds and watch them grow, as if they were doused with a sea of miracle grow! God seeds change lives. God bless you!

Love, Red

Dear you,

Stop letting others dictate your self-confidence and/or worth. Most importantly, stop allowing self-imposed doubt to stand in the way of you achieving what God has planned, and positioned, for you; self-imposed doubt kills your drive in bringing life to your dreams. Remember, some dreams are more than fantasy; they are inception seeds that God has provided for you to plant and nurture to reap an abundant life harvest.

Love, Red

Dear you,

Many, if not all, of us have experienced hate, physical attacks, verbal attacks and substantial persecution for simply being who we are as people. Don't let these attacks get or keep you down; you're worthy and can proudly hold your head up and shoulders back. Don't' permit hate to destroy your capability to love; for love escalates far above hate. I encourage you to believe in yourself and recognize the incredible value you add and that you have the power to endure through the gift of the Holy Spirit. We must value the prominence of faith and withstand this ride of life through the essence of hope. First Corinthians 13:7 says, "Love never gives up, never loses faith, is always hopeful, and endures through every circumstance." Be thankful for the gift of love. God bless you!

Love, Red

DEAR YOU

Dear you,

Throughout life, you will encounter dark moments from time to time. I encourage you to remember that even in the darkest depths, a simple spark illuminates the way. Be the light and feed your spark, as you overcome these darkness laden situations; yes, you can do it! Pop your collar and stand tall, even in the darkest of hours; for the light of your spark will never fade when you continue to head the right way. Steadily get after the light, the light of Christ. Luke 1:78–79 says, "Because of God's tender mercy, the morning light from heaven is about to break upon us, to give light to those who sit in darkness and in the shadow of death, and to guide us to the path of peace." Follow His light, find peace. God bless you!

Love, Red

Dear you,

Be courageous, rise victorious and lead the way! Yes, you can and yes, you will! Be that person that stands on the front line instead of just being a watcher on the sidelines. Your spoken word to others is so important. Why? Because with it, you either lift or tear down; the output of your word, eventually, shows who you are on the inside. Wisely put, let your yes be yes and your no be no (Matthew 5:37); stay steady on the course of right and apply Deuteronomy 31:6, which says, "So be strong and courageous! Do not be afraid and do not panic before them. For the Lord your God will personally go ahead of you. He will neither fail you nor abandon you." You got this and are NEVER ALONE! So GET AFTER THAT VICTORY! God bless you!

Love, Red

Dear you,

Although you laugh, are you okay? Although you smile, are you really smiling, or is it a mask? Only you can truthfully answer that. It's what lies beneath the exterior, far beyond the masks, that empowers effective emotional connections and direct motivation; yes, some level of emotional connection is required to fully understand yourself, let alone others. It's through this connection that enables you to exercise discernment; discernment to see beyond the thin lines of life. I encourage you to see beyond what your physical eyes can see, as well as between the thin lines of life, as you reach beyond the exterior in your pursuit of truly knowing yourself, as well as others. Don't always believe what you see, find out what lies beneath the surface. "Do your best to present yourself to God as one approved, a worker who has no need to be ashamed, rightly handling the word of truth" (2 Timothy 2:15). God bless you.

Love, Red

Dear you,

When you're going through a life storm, laughter, uncontrollable laughter, is so good for the soul. Yes, experiencing that peace, joy and happiness beyond understanding, is possible; it's possible through the power of the Holy Spirit. In fact, being high on the Holy Spirit is life-changing; when you think things are impossible, He tells you, "Relax, I'm in the midst of your battles and where you think it's impossible, He simply splits the word out saying, I'm possible." I encourage you to apply Philippians 4:6–7 and refocus your negativity, turn it into laughter; a laughter founded on the peace and high of the Holy Spirit! God bless you!

Love, Red

Dear you,

Respect for yourself is required if you want others to respect you. In fact, how you respond to the challenges of life demonstrates your level of self-respect. Keep fighting for what's right in your life; you, yes you, are strong and empowered to keep climbing above defeat. You are valuable, so have no fear to elevate your self-esteem. Once you elevate yourself internally, you enable the defining ability to physically elevate to new heights. Philippians 4:13, proof that you can, says, "For I can do everything through Christ, who gives me strength." God bless you!

Love, Red

Dear you,

Are you a contributor to the BIG picture? Short answer is "yes." This applies to many aspects of life…think about it…both spiritually and earthly. Never underestimate your role on the team you serve, but rather do the best at whatever job it is you have. Why? Because it's important in support of the BIG picture; you must realize that an important facet to team balance is not to look down on someone that sits at a different level, because there is someone who sits at a higher level than you. So remember, the key to successful support of the BIG picture is to capitalize on each other's core competencies to create synergy! After all, keeping the wheel turning in balanced rotation requires teamwork. I challenge you to embrace your role in regard to the BIG picture and to apply Colossians 3:23: "Work willingly at whatever you do, as though you were working for the Lord rather than for people." May God bless you and yours today in EVERY ASPECT! See you soon.

Love, Red

Dear you,

Family is such an awesome gift and should be considered an honor to have. You see, you have family you didn't choose and then you have the family you chose. Loving both is rare, but when you do a certain level of joy is found that few tend to experience in this life. Why is this? Well, financial, earthly, and many other statuses drive family atmospheres versus the core values of Jesus and love. A mix of Jesus and love keeps families solid and sound. Jesus is the number one core value that helps keep your family whole and allows you to show love amidst any of life's trials. Stay focused on serving Him and lead your family as read in Joshua 24:15b, "But as for me and my family, we will serve the Lord." Allow Him to lead you as you lead your family. Don't' be afraid to introduce your family to Jesus. God bless you today and may He watch over all aspects of your life!

Love, Red

Dear you,

Stand on the promises of God; it's in your actions where the hard work resides. I encourage you to put in the work needed so your actions fulfill your words. Focus on the amazing that God has allowed in your life, those things that just absolutely amaze you! Yes, we all have bad, or will face bad, but we, also, all have good. The attention you give to either one determines, which will be greater; let the amazing stomp out the bad. It's through His promises where you escape the bad, overcoming life's obstacles. Second Peter 1:4 says, "And because of His glory and excellence, He has given us great and precious promises. These are the promises that enable you to share His divine nature and escape the world's corruption caused by human desires." So stay inspired to victoriously stand on the promises of God; you can do it! God bless you.

Love, Red

DEAR YOU

Dear you,

Don't sacrifice your family in the pursuit of life. One day your ride of life will slow down; if you look to your left and right and have no one to share life with you paid too high a price in your pursuit. To be loved, and to have someone to love, is not replaceable no matter what some think. I encourage you to cherish the truth found in 1 Corinthians 13:13, which says, "Three things will last forever—faith, hope, and love—and the greatest of these is love." Stay strong in your faith, know that your hope is in God and that you can love because He first loved you! God bless you!

Love, Red

Dear you,

You hear so much about the problems in the government, turmoil on the streets, hate, economic instability, biased integrity, and so much more negativity that you can see that the morals of days past have changed, creating a new reality for you and me. People ask where God is, why He hasn't intervened; He has intervened by saving and using you. He was, is and will be here for you, throughout eternity. What is, is what it is; supported by aged, yet relevant, prophetic proverbs. In fact, one of those solid proverbs found in 28:2 says, "When there is moral rot within a nation, its government topples easily. But wise and knowledgeable leaders bring stability." For those of us that believe in God we find the truth in praying for God to be put back into our nation. However, we must realize that our new reality is filled with many denying God along with downward spiraling morals, and many choosing to accept life through practicalities and weak instabilities rather than the strength of God's stability. Pray for your family, for your leaders and your Nation; pray For God to be brought back as the true cornerstone of stability. God bless you.

Love, Red

Dear you,

Are you, or someone you know, struggling? Maybe it's work issues, financial issues, health issues, family issues, addiction issues, stress, or even some tension with a coworker. Just know that you are not alone. We all face similar issues along this ride of life. I want you to know that nothing…I REPEAT…nothing, that comes your way, is beyond the course of what others have had to face, as they steadily overcame the difficulties. How you choose to deal with it is up to you. Be inspired by 1 Corinthians 10:13, which basically says that you need to remember that God will never let you down. He knows your limits and is always here to help you through it; whatever it is you face. Well, I leave you with this, remember that you have a God that is more powerful than all the insults, hardships, persecutions, stresses, troubles, addictions, EVERYTHING. Nothing is too big for God! Praying for you today! God bless you!

Love, Red

Dear you,

Listening to the harmony among the birds, watching the lizards and snakes scurry, the squirrels chasing each other around, and the sound of water trickling, makes you realize how therapeutic and cool nature truly is. Job 12:7–8, 10 says, "Just ask the animals, and they will teach you. Ask the birds of the sky, and they will tell you. Speak to the earth, and it will instruct you. Let the fish in the sea speak to you. For the life of every living thing is in his hand, and the breath of every human being." Remember that God's answers are wiser than our prayers. When you put your life in His hands, you can experience a peace in your heart. I encourage you to live life as if the best has yet to be. See you soon!

Love, Red

Dear you,

A pendulum must stay balanced, as it sways back and forth, for the clock to tick. If the pendulum gets off balance, it stops, and the clock becomes nothing more than an idle decoration; no longer effective. The point? The pendulum represents life; balance is required to remain effective. Yes, balance requires hard work, but sustaining balance requires dedication and commitment. Ecclesiastes 3:1–8 reminds you that there is a season and time for all things. Stay balanced…don't lead yourself to becoming an idle pendulum. You can do it! God bless you!

Love, Red

Dear you,

Today is here, tomorrow may not come, but if it does, what you do today impacts your tomorrow. I encourage you to stay focused on being at your best every day in whatever it is you do, in whatever job you have and in whatever situations you face; influence your tomorrow by fully living today by applying Deuteronomy 31:6, which says, "So be strong and courageous! Do not be afraid and do not panic before them. For the LORD your God will personally go ahead of you. He will neither fail you nor abandon you." WOW! You have been empowered by a life changing God! God bless you!

Love, Red

Dear you,

Many people are facing uncertainty and/or feeling hopeless; maybe it's you. Truth is that the feeling as if no light at the end of the tunnel exists is real, making you feel that the fight for life and light has flown away on the last metaphorical flight. If you truly love yourself and others, do something about it. What can you do? Be a fortress of mental and/or physical strength, a refuge so to speak, for somebody. Everybody is, and needs, somebody, even those you might consider to be a nobody. Spiritually, God is your fortress, He is your light and steadily, for you, fights. I encourage each you to follow in His example to be the best earthly fortress for one another. Psalm 18:2 says, "The Lord is my rock, my fortress, and my savior; my God is my rock, in whom I find protection. He is my shield, the power that saves me, and my place of safety." Penetrate the world and those within your circle with the example God has left you. Increase your mental and physical strength through Him and be somebody to even the lowest nobody. God bless you and may He strengthen and inspire all aspects of your life.

Love, Red

Dear you,

How is your spiritual toolbox coming along? We all face mean people, tough and ugly situations, hurt, etc.; how we deal with it shows our character. Today, I challenge you to add forgiveness to your toolbox, which is referenced at last eighty-nine times in the Bible. You know, when you don't forgive you are setting yourself up for mechanical spiritual failure. That ole bitterness sets in like a bad case of oil leaks. Over time, if not fixed, you ruin your motor. Same goes for your spiritual walk and testimony. That ole bitterness may not affect you early on, but overtime it breaks you down and hardens your heart. Just remember, as read in Colossians 3:13, Christ forgave you... He died for you, which is why you must exercise the spiritual tool of forgiveness. Don't you truly want your reflection to be that of Him? Who do you need to forgive? Praying for God's blessings to be upon you. Forgive, you can do it.

Love, Red

Dear you,

Be bold, take the plunge—the plunge of bringing your unseen dreams, relationships, and faith alive. Having faith in the unseen, like that in God, requires boldness and allows you to lead yourself to experiencing the unseen things being seen; see, through the effects of the plunge. Fear destroys, faith leads to hope, hope leads to courage, and courage leads to the creation of life in things unseen. You mustn't fear the plunge, but rather strive to become the best leader in the jump by consistently seeking the unseen with the intent of bringing those dreams to the forefront so all can be seen. I leave you with a solid Proverb found in 12:24a, "Work hard and become a Leader." I encourage you to live life, live it well and die right. God bless you!

Love, Red

Dear you,

Inherent to life is the ability to be the living illustration. Right now, yes right now, say, "I'M ALIVE and am RISING to new HEIGHTS and even from the ashes I rise at my best to influence the rest!" Did you say it? Now, repeat it and believe it. You, first, must speak life into your life before you can truly influence life. Do you have a vision? Do you want to see your relationships grow? I encourage you to launch your vision by simply living out truth; show the way and always love and cherish God, the ultimate illustration. From experience, I know that once your attitude and actions are aligned with the right living illustration, you will positively impact your world, which naturally brings about positive and deeper growth to your life. Stay reconciled with God as you demonstrate the power of Him in your life illustration. "For God was in Christ, reconciling the world to himself, no longer counting people's sins against them. And he gave us this wonderful message of reconciliation. So we are Christ's ambassadors; God is making his appeal through us. We speak for Christ when we plead, "Come back to God!" (2 Corinthians 5:19–20). God bless you!

Love, Red

DEAR YOU

Dear you,

You are important, never doubt that, and know that the mania of your past does not have to define who you are today. However, your past impressions left can only be overcome by your consistent present way of life. I mean look at David in the Bible…he had a man murdered all because he wanted his wife (2 Samuel 11)…but he changed, repented, and is known as a man after God's own heart (Acts 13:22). What's the point? You are important because you still are alive, and God has a purpose for you to fulfill. Do not let your past stop you from giving your life back to Him. There will no doubt be those leery of your change. Why? Because first impressions are sometimes hard to overcome. The key is to show that your past life is dead and gone. How? By showing that your life reflects the Holy Spirit within you. Be blessed and be a blessing to someone today. Remember, nobodies are somebodies to someone! God bless you!

Love, Red

Dear you,

It's no surprise, when we don't stay tuned up, that the greatest, strongest, and best fall. Meaning, self-maintenance is required from time to time to stay victorious, because what you do reflects on what you get, and what you put into this life matters. You must steadily improve and strengthen yourself to keep your life driven with a God purpose; maintenance and discipline followed by dedication should be a few of your key drivers. You learn in Galatians 6:7–8 that we will reap what we sow, which applies to all aspects of life. I leave you with 1 Corinthians 10:12, "If you think you are standing strong, be careful not to fall." Stay focused on Him. God bless you!

Love, Red

Dear you,

Faith is tested during the wait. From experience, I know this all too well; over time, I have learned to remind myself of Job; he waited and never lost his faith. I encourage you to instill the same reminder when facing the "wait" and pair it with the reward found in Isaiah 40:31, "But those who trust in the Lord will find new strength. They will soar high on wings like eagles. They will run and not grow weary. They will walk and not faint." Somethings are worth the patience to ride out the wait to strengthen your faith. God bless you.

Love, Red

DEAR YOU

Dear you,

You are not insignificant! Let nothing stand in your way, not even yourself; any obstacle can be overcome and utterly defeated by pure will if it be in God's will. So don't be clouded by your own judgment; overcome yourself and the world is yours. When you feel less important than the next, remember…you are highly favored by the Living God; always, stay at your best as you influence the rest! Believe that you can bounce back from adversity. Yes, you will build and enable your mental and physical strength. You will tap into your optimal performance, you will apply strong leadership, and you will stay determined in your life's goal achievement. Bottom line is to use your free will to say, "I WILL"! First Peter 4:10–11 says, "God has given each of you a gift from his great variety of spiritual gifts. Use them well to serve one another. Do you have the gift of speaking? Then speak as though God himself were speaking through you. Do you have the gift of helping others? Do it with all the strength and energy that God supplies. Then everything you do will bring glory to God through Jesus Christ. All glory and power to him forever and ever! Amen." Stay solid and the world is yours, especially with God leading your ride! God bless you!

Love, Red

Dear you,

Do you have it in you? "Have what?" you say. Commitment. Commitment requires dedication throughout the good and bad; commitment to stand at the ready for anything life throws your way. You will face moments of discouragement in this life, but it's your commitment and dedication that fuels your endurance; through both, the good and bad, your level of commitment defines your character. This life is what you choose to make it; endure and seize all it has to offer! Stay committed to success, not only because it's right, but because you know that our God of grace strengthens and guides you, as you stand at the ready as a mighty warrior! "Don't be afraid, for I am with you. Don't be discouraged, for I am your God. I will strengthen you and help you" (Isaiah 41:10). Get out there and experience a day like never before, to feel the best you have ever felt and to achieve what you have been working so hard toward. Stay committed! God bless you!

Love, Red

Dear you,

Wisdom is a culmination of your past and present life lessons learned. Wisdom enables you to build a better future, as you see beyond what your eyes can see; it leads to trust, loyalty, and knowledge. For without trust you have no loyalty; without loyalty you have no, nor get, real knowledge. You must continue to build your inner house in part with a foundation of wisdom; seek others who have wisdom and learn, and then, teach the up and coming, you love, how important seeking, not only earthly wisdom, the Wisdom of God really is. A solid Proverb found in 24:3–7 says, "By wisdom a house is built, and by understanding it is established; by knowledge the rooms are filled with all precious and pleasant riches. A wise man is full of strength, and a man of knowledge enhances his might, for by wise guidance you can wage your war, and in abundance of counselors there is victory." Victory is yours to be had; up to you to RISE UP and get after it. God bless you!

Love, Red

Dear you,

If you want a friend you got to be a friend. If you never put yourself out there, within reason, or reach back when reached to then don't expect folks to keep reaching out to you. Relationships are two-way streets. I encourage you to respond in ways you want to be responded to, be the example you want others to be. Why? Because focusing on a being a better, stronger and successful you, strengthens and builds the success in your life. Remember a servant heart is meant to get stronger. A successful person understands the importance and required value of maintaining a servant's attitude within your heart, which is displayed by your actions. I leave you with Matthew 20:28 which says, "For even the Son of Man came not to be served but to serve others and to give His life as a ransom for many." Be a friend, a godly friend. God bless you!

Love, Red

Dear you,

See beyond what you can see; open your inner eyes and experience true reality. A wise person knows that perceptions change, realities evolve. Are you facing a strenuous situation? Maybe it's a situation with another person, maybe it's a decision that tremendously affects your future, or maybe it's righting a wrong. Whatever the "MAYBE" is to you, you can succeed. In 1 Samuel 17 we recount the remarkable story of David and Goliath. David was a scrawny young boy and Goliath was an overall superior strength kind of guy; we all know both types. Goliath just knew he would win, but David knew he had God. David didn't just say he would fight him, he said he would KILL HIM. Verse 46 says, "Today the Lord will conquer you, and I will kill you and cut off your head. And then I will give the dead bodies of your men to the birds and wild animals, and the whole world will know that there is a God in Israel!" I encourage you to stand up against your personal Goliaths, see beyond what you can physically see and show that God is ALIVE AND REAL! Stand ready; God bless you!

Love, Red

Dear you,

Don't be defeated, do not let people or circumstances rob you of your joy; your joy comes from within. Rise up, YES, Rise up! Muster that inner drive to rise, overcome and succeed! It's up to you to succeed as the victor! So drive on and do it, make it happen! Romans 8:28 says, "And we know that God causes everything to work together for the good of those who love God and are called according to His purpose for them." Believe in yourself and RISE UP! God bless you. BTW. YOU CAN DO IT!

Love, Red

DEAR YOU

Dear you,

Stomp out that negativity and shade thrown at you by remaining humble. What? Yes, there is strength in remaining humble. You're probably saying, "I'll stomp it alright, but not by being humble! You just don't know where I work or who or what I am dealing with! You just don't know the amount of shade being thrown at me or how thick the negativity is. So how can I stay humble?" Well, from my experience, regardless of the situation (good or bad) you still learn; you learn how, and how not, to act, and how, and how not, to treat others. I encourage you to remember that you can only control you; respond in the ways you want to be responded to, be the example of the person you want others to be. Maybe…just maybe…your positivity and humble attitude will rub off on someone. Try it. Focus on a better and successful you; build yourself up with a foundation sealed in sincere humbleness. Hard? Yes, but Jesus was a true example of this concept. I leave you with Matthew 20:28, which says, "For even the Son of Man came not to be served but to serve others and to give His life as a ransom for many." May God watch over and bless you!

Love, Red

Dear you,

Yes, at times, life will throw things your way making you feel like there is no tomorrow. Your patience, temper, character…your life will be tested. Staying in control, despite the good or bad and/or the times when people test your patience, is a direct reflection of your inner strength and character; stay strong. I encourage you to give all your trials and problems to God and seek His wisdom; use the tool of discernment. Remember, even when answers seem far away you're not alone. Yes, it's hard, but from my personal experience the pain and patience is worth the reward. EVERYTHING is possible through Christ and NOTHING is IMPOSSIBLE. Hit up 1 Corinthians 10:13 and Philippians 4:13, for they are some great hip pocket references. Now smile, as you get after today, and never doubt that you can always become a better and stronger you! God bless you!

Love, Red

Dear you,

Don't settle for mediocre, be GREAT! Part of being great is teaching what you know to the up and coming, for a great leader understands the importance of showing and teaching the way! Even the most seasoned leaders understand that they still have the capability to learn something new and that there is more power in sharing knowledge than keeping it bottled inside. The key is that you must practice what you teach and involve the up and coming if you want the lesson to stick. Remember, a lesson learned is worth a lesson shared. Apply Romans 15:2, which says, "We should help others do what is right and build them up in the Lord." Now get out there and get after it! Make a difference in this world, build your up and coming up with the knowledge capable of growing into wisdom. May God bless you!

Love, Red

DEAR YOU

Dear you,

As a leader of self and/or team your words and actions impact, not only yourself, but those you encounter along the way. Your words mean nothing if you never bring them to life through actions, and your actions mixed with minced words can cause situations to fall apart, leaving possible solutions untouched. We have the freedom of choice; allow your words to be brought to life through your actions. For example, I say it and choose to never give up on another, and encourage you to consider choosing the same. Why? Because everyone, hits a low spot from time to time and needs somebody to simply encourage them, rather than disparage their comeback. Kicking someone while they are down is cowardly; where standing toe to toe establishes confidence and leads to lessons learned. Hate grows, if you allow it. Anger takes over, if you allow it. Rage destroys yourself and others, if you allow it. However, the opposite of those will happen as well, if you allow it. You have the freedom to choose; I humbly suggest you choose wisely and consider the consequences of your choices. Remember, one day you could be the one down and out and need the help. I encourage each you to use our freedom of choice to better yourself and those you encounter along the way. Be remembered as one who uses your freedom to build up, rather than destroy, and love, rather than hate. Galatians 5:13–15 in the MSG version hits home. "It is absolutely clear that God has called you to a free life. Just make sure that you don't use this freedom as an excuse to do whatever you want to do and destroy your freedom. Rather, use your freedom to serve one another in love; that's how freedom grows. For everything we know about God's Word is summed up in a single sentence: Love others as you love yourself. That's an act of true freedom. If you bite and ravage each other, watch out—in no time at all you will be annihilating each other, and where will your precious freedom be then?" Let your action match your words. God bless you!

Love, Red

Dear you,

Your actions lead to reactions, just as your reactions cause actions. As part of self-assessment, I encourage you to ask yourself, "Do my actions and/or reactions show strength or weakness in my commitments?" Why? Because commitment earns respect; success requires it. With God your commitment is backed up by His power and what you've committed to do has a better chance of happening if you are committed in putting Him in charge of your plans. Don't just be satisfied in life be gratified; your commitment to put Him first allows a steady course for the commitments you make to man. Proverbs 16:3 says, "Commit your actions to the Lord, and your plans will succeed." Stay steady, committed, and stand ready. God bless you!

Love, Red

Dear you,

RISE UP, STEP UP and ROLL ON! Along the way make someone's day today! Why? To show a bit of love…that's why. Have you ever heard, "They have fallen way too many times and will never get back on their feet, there's just no hope for them? They don't even stand by their word"? Yea, I've heard it to. Well, I don't believe in giving up on folks. Lord knows many folks will give up on you, but God never does! Wrongs can be forgiven or made right. Addictions can be a thing of the past. Depression can be set free. Jobs can be got. Bottom line is that your life can and will turn around if you want it to. How? God. God's already showed up, He's waiting on you to grow up! Let the past go and start new with Him. "For God is not unjust. He will not forget how hard you have worked for him and how you have shown your love to him by caring for others…keep on loving others as long as life lasts, in order to make certain that what you hope for will come true" (Hebrews 6:10–11). God bless you! Never give up!

Love, Red

Dear you,

Every road you have taken has lead you to today. Yes, at times, those roads were tough, but you are still standing. You do your best to hold it all together, even when the struggle is real and appears to have no end. Yes, you do, and will have, moments where you think you are going strong and then, BAM, life just knocks you down to the ground. So what sets you apart? Your character and strength, for they shine at your lowest moments. It's in those moments, where you are barely hanging on to the little you got left, but remain strong when others fall weak, that you shine the brightest. I encourage you to be reminded that even the smallest steps in life have purpose, and, with each step, stay committed in resting and waiting on the Lord. Psalm 37:16 says, "A little that a righteous man hath is better than the riches of many wicked." Keep on keeping on because you're held in the hand of God. God bless you!

Love, Red

Dear you,

One of the worst things you can do to someone is to lie to them, especially to yourself. For when you are biased, lie or lazy you compromise you, damaging your values and reputation. I encourage you to create synergy by maintaining integrity, rather than misery spawned by lies. A solid Proverb found in 19:9 says, "A false witness will not go unpunished, and a liar will be destroyed." The truth spawns triumph!

Love, Red

Dear you,

Whatever is negatively impacting you, let it go! Whatever stress, task, worry, whatever it is, that is affecting you in unhealthy ways, LET IT GO! Life is so short, and death is destined to come for us all, so, don't let stress or negativity run your life. I encourage to you STAND strong, even if only through His strength, stand strong. We serve a mighty God that has more than enough love and strength for you to get you through this day, to get you through the tasks, to enable positive rotations; stay calm and strong. "For the Lord your God is living among you. He is a mighty savior. He will take delight in you with gladness. With his love, he will calm all your fears. He will rejoice over you with joyful songs" (Zephaniah 3:17). The journey is greater when you let it go. God bless you today. Live life, live it well and die right.

Love, Red

Dear you,

Authenticity of a legacy; keep it real. Being authentic builds trust; being authentic, rather than synthetic, allows your legacy to last a lifetime. I encourage you to apply authenticity to your ride of life; because if you want authentic success, authentic relationships, then you, yourself, first must be authentic in all aspects of your life. A solid Proverb found in 12:19 says, "Truthful words stand the test of time, but lies are soon exposed." Lead from the front and exemplify truth; be authentic. Let the authenticity of your legacy be worthy to talk about. God bless you today!

Love, Red

Dear you,

Engaging in conversation is inevitable; it's how you choose to impact the conversation that will be remembered. A fundamental principle is that the power of your response directly influences the response you receive, which is why it's imperative, not to mention advantageous, to respond, both, wisely and positively. I encourage you to think before you respond, which will help lead you in cultivating a conversation style built on noteworthy fundamental principles. I leave you with a solid Proverb found in 15:1, "A gentle answer deflects anger, but harsh words make tempers flare." Impact your relationships with positive growth, rather than leaving them jaded, full of exhausted negativity. God bless you!

Love, Red

Dear you,

Up to you to choose what kind of day you are going to have. Let Almighty God, inspire you; spend some time in His sixty-six loves letters, the Bible! Through Him your day should be filled with happiness, prayer and thankfulness. In fact each of these are found in 1 Thessalonians 5:16–18: "Always be joyful. Never stop praying. Be thankful in all circumstances, for this is God's will for you who belong to Christ Jesus." So I reassure you to get after it, and pray for your day to be super fantastic in all aspects. God bless you!

Love, Red

Dear you,

It's up to you to maintain the dedication to lead yourself through the doors of life with forward momentum, overcoming each and every objective life throws your way. A defining factor is your commitment to nurture and grow your inner strength. Whatever it is you are facing…you…yes you, have been enabled with the courage and strength to persevere. An honorable legacy is a legacy fueled in part with, not only commitment but, the strength of dedication to consistently follow through and push forward each and every day. So as you get after the day, keep on keeping on, push forward and be successful. Colossians 3:17 says, "Whatever you do or say, do it as a representative of the Lord Jesus, giving thanks through him to God the Father." God bless you!

Love, Red

Dear you,

Sometimes you travel by the light of day and sometimes through the darkness of the night. Don't let the darkness of night land you in the bottom of life's abyss, where the inner monsters are mighty and great. Light is symbolic to the light implanted in you by the power of Christ, with darkness being the sin that holds you deep down in the perilous abyss, and the monsters are the negative things you allow to drive your thoughts and actions. I encourage you to defeat your monsters by consistently searching the light of Christ. I believe in you and know that you will emerge and soar out of life's abyss. John 8:12 confirms it, "I am the light of the world. If you follow me, you won't have to walk in darkness, because you will have the light that leads to life." God bless you!

Love, Red

DEAR YOU

Dear you,

Self-control is an essential tool in your life toolbox; use it. Don't let negative input cause you to produce negative output. Yes, at times, things seem unbearable, wrong or simply unfair; these things can even light that fire of rage within your soul, but you must hold on and don't' give that much control of your emotions away to another. Yes, life does gets tough from time to time; I encourage you to stay in control of your life, protect yourself and never give up; steadily exercise the gift of self-control. As a child of God, you have Him right here with you fighting for you in ways you may never realize. Through Him you can…rejoice in hope, be patient in tribulation, be constant in prayer and, in turn, help show another the way (Romans 12:12–13). God bless you!

Love, Red

Dear you,

From time to time, even the best of the best will have dark and broken moments that can spiral out of control. Hence the importance in never underestimating the power of a listening ear and a kind word, along with a strong embrace. Just be careful not to push people away, but rather take the time to listen and love, because when you push them away you could be pushing them straight to their death. If you stay quiet nothing ever changes and remember everybody is a somebody. God bless you!

Love, Red

Dear you,

You ready, ready for some hope and joy? Shout it! "I'M READY!" It doesn't matter what you look like, what you wear, how much money you have, or don't have, you're a somebody, an important somebody that God loves. Yes, you must know that you are a somebody even if others treat you like a nobody. This awesome and confident joy comes from the Lord; don't let nothing rob you of that inner joy, but rather let it rub off on those you encounter along the way. I pray that your day is solid and that, as found in Romans 15:13, you allow God to fill you with joy and peace. After all, hope abounds in joy; think about it. God bless you!

Love, Red

Dear you,

Ever feel like your life is overwhelming, leaving you feeling as if, no matter how hard you try, you are living on a bed of quick sand? I know I have. In fact it's safe to say that most of us have had and will have overwhelming situations. The beautiful thing is that each of us can overcome them. How? God will make a way, yes, a way! HE parted the Red Sea, HE breathed life into the valley of dead bones, HE caused the walls of Jericho to fall after seven days and, most importantly, HE died and rose again. The list can go on and on, so there is no doubt that HE has us covered for a lifetime. "I am the Alpha and the Omega," says the Lord God, "who is and who was and who is to come, the Almighty" (Revelation 1:8). So stomp out fear and overcome by giving it all to God; just make sure to do your part and hold on! God bless you!

Love, Red

DEAR YOU

Dear you,

Listen, learn, and teach; do your part...yes, you have a part. "Listen to advice and accept instruction, that you may gain wisdom in the future" (Proverbs 19:20). I repeat, listen, learn and teach in order to gain wisdom from those who have gone before you. Why? Growth, intelligence, a better future...that's why. "An intelligent heart acquires knowledge, and the ear of the wise seeks knowledge" (Proverbs 18:15). The point? All aspects of life require you to exercise wisdom gained from the knowledge and instructions received. If you stay quiet and do nothing then nothing changes. Do your part to listen, learn, and teach. God bless you!

Love, Red

Dear you,

Are you a 3D kind of person? You know, 3D; determined, dedicated and dependable. Let the positivity of being 3D be founded and grounded in your soul, as it radiates to all those you encounter today! Remember, growth requires self-growth, which directly requires your involvement, determination, and dedication. You are worth it, John 3:16 confirms it. So be dependable, as you depend on God to fulfill His promises through you! Simply, stay at your best wherever you are in this thing called life and let your light shine! God bless you!

Love, Red

Dear you,

The literary work, such as Moby Dick, was relevant to the success of Herman Melville. God is just as relevant to the success of your life; for your career, your family, your relationships all become infected with a touch of God once you allow Him to infect you. Never doubt how worthy and important you are in influencing your circle, BE CONTAGIOUS with your infection! Do something extraordinary that impacts a life and keep strengthening your legacy each second of each minute; allow your reputation and legacy to survive a lifetime. Have a great day, and allow the value of 1 Peter 1:18–19 to resonate in your infection! "For you know that God paid a ransom to save you from the empty life you inherited from your ancestors. And it was not paid with mere gold or silver, which lose their value. It was the precious blood of Christ, the sinless, spotless Lamb of God." God bless you!

Love, Red

Dear you,

Family! What was, is not what is, and, what will be, is yet to be. So appreciate the here and now, breathe, ride hard and rest easy. Yes, you are going to experience ups and downs and periodical flats in your wheel of life, but, whatever happens, breathe. WHAT? That's right, breathe. You feel that? You are ALIVE, your wheel of life is still a turning, which means you have another opportunity to be a Brother's Keeper, a solid man, another chance to strengthen your legacy. For those spiritually inclined, this also means that God isn't done with you yet! No matter your burden, no matter your situation, HE is right here with you; so rest in HIM. Matthew 11:30 says, "For my yoke is easy, and my burden is light." The point? Appreciate the here and now, breathe, work hard and rest easy! Let your wheel of life yield positive rotation, led by balance, and enjoy the ride to a great final destination!

Love, Red

DEAR YOU

Dear you,

Let your heart beat again. Your heart will be broken more than once in life, now that's a fact. No worries, it's going to be okay, yes, it will be okay…so let your heart beat again. Psalm 34:18 says, "The Lord is close to the brokenhearted; He rescues those whose spirits are crushed." Yesterday can't be undone, but today is here and now; hence the importance of living for today. Being selfless starts with you taking care of you…don't be selfish to your heart. I encourage each of us to stay open to allowing the hurts in our lives to be mended… for each of us to let our heart beat again. If you start to doubt that it will beat again, really give it God. John 14:13 says, "You can ask for anything in my name, and I will do it, so that the Son can bring glory to the Father." He never changes; same yesterday, today and forever. So be proud of yourself and the contributions you make and LET YOUR HEART BEAT AGAIN. You, yes YOU, add value! God bless you!

Love, Red

Dear you,

After watching an episode of Moonshiners, I began to think about the power of fire. Just like in making shine, where fire is required, there needs to be that spiritual fire in our lives. Think about it, fire, a proven gift through the ages, is required to brew the best of anything; this is why we must nurture and grow the fire within our soul. After all, that spiritual fire is a gift from God and creates that burning desire to shine the strongest for Him, which will be evident to those on our team, as well as those we encounter along the way. The stronger the fire and how you control the fire, the stronger the shine. The stronger the spiritual fire and how you grow the fire, the stronger you will shine for Him, making impacts that matter in all aspects of your life. I encourage you to ignite your inner fire and brew the best in you, yielding your strongest shine! Yes indeed, through Him, you will yield the strongest shine with solid proof. I leave you with Hebrews 12:29. "For our God is a consuming fire." Let Him consume you and mold you into the best you! God bless you.

Love, Red

DEAR YOU

Dear you,

We all get caught up in life, along with all the things associated with making it successful and happy. The sad part is when someone chooses to love success or money more than the team. First Timothy 6:10 says, "For the love of money is the root of all kinds of evil. And some people, craving money, have wandered from the true faith and pierced themselves with many sorrows." I've seen many embrace this burning love of money and have watched what people will do for a dollar and how they hurt their relationships along the way to simply move up the invisible ladders of life. Many lose their peace of mind and destroy the peace found in solid teams that were once founded on respect and unified for the greater cause. In fact many teams have been destroyed because the dynamics change when people gun for the top with no regards to how they hurt their fellow team members. Nothing wrong with money, success or even climbing the ladders; it's how you go about reaching the top that defines your character. I encourage each of us to never sacrifice our relationships along the way, stay humble and lift one another up. As Zac Brown once said, "There's no dollar sign on a piece of mind…I thank God for my life and for the stars and stripes…may freedom forever fly, let it ring." God bless you!

Love, Red

Dear you,

Sometimes, you have to make sure you help yourself before you can truly help another.

Love, Red

Dear you,

Never underestimate the power in how you ride out this life. You don't live it for only you. Those outsiders, but most importantly, your Brothers and Sisters are watching. Is your ride worth emulating? Legacy is strengthened by solid actions comprised by those that really care, and want nothing but success to be born at birth, throughout the ride and a legacy to last, as the ashes travel through the wind.

Love, Red

Dear you,

Eliminate the "Manic Monday" syndrome, knock it square in the mouth and let nothing destroy your happy! Being happy is a choice, for life keeps coming at you day in and day out, and being unhappy doesn't make the problems go away. Maybe you need to evaluate the "how" by which you process your situations. I encourage you to remember what Leo Tolstoy once said, "If you want to be happy, be." Anyways, as one of God's, our time on earth isn't going to match our time in eternity. Build your foundation on Him and you will have every reason to rejoice and be happy! YES, you will gladly sing Philippians 4:4, "Rejoice in the Lord always: and again I say, Rejoice!" Now get after it and BE HAPPY! God bless you and yours!

Love, Red

Dear you,

Some of the smallest things you do for your brother and sister matter; it's the discipline found in these little things that contributes to the strength of the nation. A solid truth is that what might be small to you, might be huge to them; for example, a kind word, a helping hand, or maybe a listening ear. Remember, lifting up one another should never cease as long as you are on this ride of life. I'm reminded of what Ronald Reagan once said, "We can't help everyone, but everyone can help someone." Be there for your Brother and Sister and love by actions, not simply by words.

Love, Red

Dear you,

That emptiness, the feeling of being or having nothing, consumes many people throughout their life; I, myself, have experienced it. However, you don't have to be a victim of this vicious place in life. I encourage each of us to become the example; impact the nothing so hard that it becomes something and remember that nothing changes unless you do something. For example, when you are afforded the opportunity to positively impact your life, don't misuse or forgo the moment; it might just be the last moment you breathe. The point is, if something isn't right in your life and you do nothing, then expect nothing to ever change. It's up to you to make the required changes to turn your nothing into something! If you say you're gonna do it, do it; Ecclesiastes 5:7a says, "Talk is cheap…" Continue to believe in yourself, lift your head up, stand up straight and carry on. You can do it. Philippians 4:13 says so: "I can do all things through him who strengthens me." God bless you today.

Love, Red

Dear you,

Look in the mirror…just don't let the reflection startle you…haha. What you see is someone that is loved, is important, and has purpose; even when you feel alone, not needed, or less important than the rest you overcome by being your best! You, yes you, are important! Believe it! Let nothing negative stand in your way, as you make a positive difference today. Keep your relationships in good standing, keep your attitude on the up and up, make sure your internal wheel stays balanced and do your part in creating and maintaining harmony across your team. The cool part is that God is in it and is with you, as you stay in it to win it! I leave you with Paul's final greetings found in 2 Corinthians 13:11, "Dear brothers and sisters, I close my letter with these last words: Be joyful. Grow to maturity. Encourage each other. Live in harmony and peace. Then the God of love and peace will be with you." Believe in yourself, be at your best. God bless you!

Love, Red

Dear you,

Get to know your team. Although one laughs, are they really okay? Although one smiles, are they really smiling? Leadership requires getting past the exterior. This is key to establishing the emotional connection and direct motivation. It's the connection that enables you, as a Leader, to exercise discernment; knowing what motivates each member, as well as what is really going on beneath the surface. Erma Bombeck once said, "There is a thin line that separates laughter and pain, comedy and tragedy, humor and hurt." I encourage you to reach out and get to know the team and remember the truth found in 1 Corinthians 12:26 which says, "If one member suffers, all suffer together; if one member is honored, all rejoice together." Don't always believe what you see, find out what lies beneath the surface. Try having lunch with one another. God bless you.

Love, Red

DEAR YOU

Dear you,

Take note… The power of growth suffocates the strength of death. As many do, I enjoy a hot cup of coffee early in morning, as I pray to and thank God, preparing for the day. As spring rolls out, the mornings are brighter and signs of life travel through the woods; there is a peace in watching the trees and plants sprout new life. Mixed with new life, in the midst of the woods, I have been watching this tree, which is predominantly dead from the trunk up; it is a tree that you would think would eventually need cut down, seeing as how it appeared to have no visible signs of life. The limbs are brittle and the trunk sounds hollow with no obvious appearance of buds ready to grow; however, right in the middle of what seemed dead, comes along a bud, followed by another, which have now began to grow. What once appeared dead is being consumed with new growth, a direct sign of life. My, my…how symbolic this is to our life here on earth. For when we think things in our life are dying or dead, along comes the power of growth and new life. Yes, in the midst of our teams, to our families, relationships, churches, country, our "whatever" comes the power of growth, reviving us, enabling us and empowering us. This power of growth and life is better known as Jesus; He takes what once appeared dead and, if invited, breathes new life into us, which becomes visibly apparent in all aspects of our life. Second Corinthians 5:17 says, "Therefore, if anyone is in Christ, he is a new creation. The old has passed away; behold, the new has come." So I encourage you to seek Him, allow Him to fill you with LIFE. For whatever aspects of your life appear dead, needing a fresh start, He is able to suffocate the power of death, because HE IS LIFE. Do you have Him in yours? God bless you!

Love, Red

Dear you,

Hate, a nasty trait, so heavily present all over the globe. Just listen to the radio, watch a little TV, tune in to a pod cast, read a blog, etc.… and you inevitably encounter various stories fueled by hate. One of the most important things you can do is to love. Yes, LOVE! First Corinthians 13:13 says, "Three things will last forever—faith, hope, and love—and the greatest of these is love." I encourage each of us to never doubt the strength found in love, a direct contributor to positive relationships, and let today be the beginning of restoration of those broken relationships by using love as a tool to reconcile any hate and/or differences responsible for tearing the relationships apart. Legacy is strengthened by acts of love; to be remembered is up to you. Live life, live it well and die right. God bless you today!

Love, Red

Dear you,

A wise person knows that you never stop learning or building that toolbox of life; some things learned you never throw away. Yes, it is important to keep your life toolbox current, but remember to hold on to those irreplaceable tools, such as wisdom, knowledge, integrity and honor. The right tools builds the right legacy. God bless you!

Love, Red

Dear you,

Can people see that you genuinely care and love? Strive to let your love been seen. For your ride of life leaves a trail; will it be one to emulate? Let your journey, not only show your love, but show just how selfless you truly are along your life journey. Because selfless leadership leads to trust, respect and loyalty. In fact a selfless leader protects, cares for and loves their family NO MATTER THE COST, leaving an example to model after. I'm reminded of the teachings found in Philippians 1:27–30, which teaches loyalty in serving God, standing strong together as a family fighting for the faith and getting through the struggles and sufferings as one body; it is a clear example of selfless leadership. I encourage you, as you twist that throttle of life, be ready to die with the right legacy and a trail worth emulating. Praying for each of you to be blessed and strong!

Love, Red

Dear you,

If you wait until you can do everything for everybody, instead of something for somebody, you'll end up doing nothing for nobody. Remember, if you stay quiet nothing changes. It starts with helping one.

Love, Red

Dear you,

…the Cross means life and gives us freedom to live a full life, enjoying what He has created. So get out and enjoy it; experience the beauty of God's creations and spread a little bit of love wherever you go!

Love, Red

Dear you,

Effective team members complete, rather than compete to the point of destroying, the team. Effective team members lift up and encourage one another, rather than trying to tear the others down and/or discredit them. Negative team members evolve, they become ineffective for the team, and, once a team is consumed by ineffective team members, the mission suffers. Which one are you, effective or ineffective? I encourage you, as a leader, to set the standard for being effective; for your success and seamless growth depends on it. I leave you with a solid Proverb found in 27:17, "As iron sharpens iron, so a friend sharpens a friend." Be effective and sharpen another. God bless you!

Love, Red

Dear you,

Take note; there is no sense in making situations worse. Sun Tzu once said, "The supreme art of war is to subdue the enemy without fighting." Some of life's best battles are ended by the other party thinking they have won, when in reality they have lost. Exodus 14:14, one of my favorite references, says, "The Lord himself will fight for you. Just stay calm." I encourage you to stay calm and in control throughout life's battles, rather than making situations worse. Allow Him to battle for, shelter and deliver you. Live with VICTORY, stand TRIUMPHANTLY and die with HONOR. God bless you and may your weekend be super fantastic!

Love, Red

Dear you,

Life's encounters along the way, the lives we inspire, the doors traveled through, each hold a part in shaping who we are today. It is in theses encounters, in the memories of those you inspire and how you handle what is faced on the other side of the door that represents who you are in this life; it is here where your legacy lives and grows. Honor your legacy by owning it, consistently focused on the mark; conquer your objectives. I leave you with what Paul said in one of his final greetings to the people, "May the grace of our Lord Jesus Christ be with you" (1 Thessalonians 5:28). God bless you!

Love, Red

Dear you,

Self-discipline is a sign of strength, triumph and honor. It has been said that one who lives without discipline dies without honor. Standing for your life necessitates discipline and determination; this self-discipline enables you to live with purpose and honor in knowing that you do not fight to die for what's wrong, but fight to die for what's right. First Peter 2:17 says, "Honor all people. Love the brotherhood. Fear God. Honor the king." I encourage you to ensure that honor is part of your life legacy. Teach it. God bless you.

Love, Red

Dear you,

Stand tall, for today is your day to grow in confidence, which is the strength of self-assurance, knowing that you are a strong you. Increased confidence leads to increased abilities, which generates increased results; it's up to you to start believing in yourself. Say, "I know I can, rather than I think I can!" I'm reminded of what Norman Vincent Peale once said, "Believe in yourself! Have faith in your abilities! Without a humble but reasonable confidence in your own powers you cannot be successful or happy." I encourage you to get after that confidence, but remember confidence mustn't be mistaken for cocky, which is an aggressive trait fueled with arrogance and ignorance, because we all know that cocky gets kicked off the blocky…so stay humble! True confidence is found in the Lord…let HIM help you. Hebrews 13:6 says, "So we can say with confidence, "The Lord is my helper, so I will have no fear. What can mere people do to me?" Simply, stay strong and don't let haters get at you; for you stand as the strongest through HIM. God bless you!

Love, Red

Dear you,

Stay encouraged, as you transform the future. Do you want strength found in team unity? Do you want to preserve and grow the up and coming with the right core values? Do you want survival and implementation of lessons learned? The answer is probably "yes"! Well, it starts with each of us being authentic in our actions. We must focus on properly leading by example, by establishing authentic vision, founded on honesty, while keeping a growth mindset built upon seamless integrity. At the end of the day it is about transformation evidenced by hard work. In other words, I encourage each of us to be a leading spoke that keeps the wheel balanced, pressing forward toward the objective with a never give up attitude. Philippians 4:13 says you can do it…through Him. God bless you.

Love, Red

DEAR YOU

Dear you,

Sometimes it feels like life just punched you in the face…a beating you will never forget. However, You have the strength to continue on and overcome; believe it. The truth is that we all have hurts, disappointments, mistakes or insecurities that we wish we could change. Some may ask, "How do you keep on keeping on?" Well, you must take time to reflect and realize that the possibility of you changing those things alone is unattainable. So is there hope? Yes, with God. When you look to God's unconditional love and mercy you will realize that through His unending power those worries, hurts, disappointments, and insecurities fade away through His power. You fight to survive through Him. He stands for you, as you stand for Him. I pray that as you continue on this ride of life that your troubles be less, your blessings be more and nothing but happiness come through your door. Just remember that only through Him comes true deliverance. It says in Colossians 2:5–7, "For though I am far away from you, my heart is with you. And I rejoice that you are living as you should and that your faith in Christ is strong. And now, just as you accepted Christ Jesus as your Lord, you must continue to follow Him. Let your roots grow down into Him, and let your lives be built on Him. Then your faith will grow strong in the truth you were taught, and you will overflow with thankfulness." God bless you and keep the fight strong.

Love, Red

Dear you,

Mentor and lift up those around you; exercise the commitment to teach. Yes, teach…I say again…teach. Why? Because the ones you teach are the ones that will keep the legacy of the life alive; you can count on that. Each day might not be everything you want to teach, or is it? Matter of perspective on how you define your reality. Today, as Paul says in Romans 15:13, "I pray that God, the source of hope, will fill you completely with joy and peace because you trust in Him." God bless you!

Love, Red

Dear you,

Be careful what you say, for your word, apart from your heart, is one of your most valuable assets. Just imagine how great this life would be if everyone meant what they said and followed through with doing what they said they would do. As a leader, of self or team, I encourage you to never compromise your word. Be a leader known to have the word as solid as a rock, rather than a word sticky and slick as sinking sand. Abraham Lincoln once said, "Better to remain silent and be thought a fool than to speak out and remove all doubt." So as we ride out this things called life, I encourage each of us to keep Proverbs 13:3 in mind, "Those who control their tongue will have a long life; opening your mouth can ruin everything." Be careful what you say. God bless you!

Love, Red

Dear you,

Today, YES TODAY, is the beginning of something great for your life; it's an opportunity you don't want to miss! I love what Milton Berle says, "If opportunity doesn't knock, build a door!" I encourage you to focus on the forward progress not the backward slide, and remember that appreciating the little things allows you to see the value in, as well as cherish, the big things. After all, He says in John 10:10b, "My purpose is to give them a rich and satisfying life." Life; embrace it, appreciate it and get after it. God bless you!

Love, Red

Dear you,

Jumping on a bandwagon, on the wrong journey, is like jumping off a cliff with no parachute, it doesn't end well. As a leader of yourself and/or team, it's crucial to assess the integrity of the bandwagons you allow yourself, or those you lead, to jump on. Sometimes you, as a leader, have to take the risks of jumping off the wagon, changing course to paths that lead you and/or your team to success. The point is that you, me, all of us are on some type of journey, and it's up to us, as leaders, to define the risks of the wagons we ride or lead. Don't' fear the risk, fear the destination of failure if the course your wagon is on is wrong. Ask yourself, "Have I jumped on a bandwagon for the wrong reasons, supporting the wrong things? Am I leading my team to imminent failure?" If so, make it a short ride, change course, take the risk of paving a new way; or stay destined to fall off the cliff with the rest. Ray Bradbury once said, "Living at risk is jumping off the cliff and building your wings on the way down." I encourage you to let your wings sprout, take flight, assess the risks and soar to success. Take a few and hit up Ephesians 3:14–21. I leave you with verse 16, "I pray that from His glorious, unlimited resources He will empower you with inner strength through His Spirit." God bless you and your journey.

Love, Red

Dear you,

Today is your day! Whatever you are facing, you are able to overcome! Whatever doubts you have, you can stomp them out and stand with confidence! Whatever is draining your energy, you can power and push through it! Now, in order to see the results of the "you can," you need to shout, "I WILL!" I encourage each of us to keep Philippians 4 in our hip pocket, as we get after the day. Now get after it and show the world your will-power to thrive and drive to make that legacy one to survive, to survive the tests of time! God bless you on this day!

Love, Red

Dear you,

Live, laugh and love today; take advantage of each second of each minute. Be remembered, not forgotten. As a "Whosoever" don't fear muddy or troubled waters, for He delivers and leads to a forever legacy, John 3:16 confirms it.

Love, Red

Dear you,

A lot can be learned from the life a little ole ant. They work hard together for the greater good of their colony and are loyal in contributing their part; they are indeed Soldiers, Soldiers preparing for their family. Comparing this to our life shows us that success requires commitment and hard work…loyal to contributing our part. I encourage each of us to ensure that we stay ready for the long haul, get the job done and stay loyal to our commitments, while we steadily work for not only our family, but as we work among God's family. For just like each ant has purpose, you and I have a profound purpose in building up our families and the Kingdom. Hit up Proverbs 6:6–11. God bless you today.

Love, Red

Dear you,

A little truth shouldn't hurt nobody. Show me. A lot of people won't believe something unless you can show them. I know you have heard the phrase, "I ain't gonna believe until I see it!" Well, when it comes to life you show those around you exactly who you are, not by words, but through your actions! You are living, breathing and heart beating proof that Jesus is so real and alive. So are your day to day actions showing the realness of Jesus? Or are you finding yourself being that stereotypical Christian…you know the parking lot Christian. What? Yes, there are parking lot Christians, which are those that live like hell until they hit the parking lot of the church; once their feet hit that parking lot ground they magically transform into this super spiritual, almost holier than thou, kinda folk, and then when church is over they go back living like hell. This sure don't make Jesus happy. He expects us to live it day by day…every day! Yes, we make mistakes, which 1 John 1:9 covers. I encourage each of us to inventory our lives and to change those areas that don't quite reflect the realness of Jesus. Clean ourselves up, so to speak. I tell ya, that when you see the power and wonder in answered prayers and God working in your situations it gives you a new found spark of heart energy! From experience, walking out life's good and bad with faith is hard sometimes, but rewarding every time. Personally, I show Him every day, not blemish free but if you ask me, "Show ME," I guarantee I can show ya. Why? Because I know that the power and wonders of God are indeed real; He shows up every day for me. Do you? Show me. Love you and pray for God to bless all aspects of your life!

Love, Red

Dear you,

Remembered or forgotten? Enemies, broken relationships, many foreseen and unforeseen battles will be faced and overcome throughout your ride of life. It's how you deal with and overcome life's challenges that contributes to, you, being either remembered or forgotten. Fight for what's right, be a warrior in your pursuit of being remembered. Paul Watson once said, "I am a warrior, and it's the way of the warrior to fight superior odds." Being defeated, giving up hope, leads to the possibility of being forgotten. Demonstrating resilience and applying the precepts of the warrior ethos to your ride of life increases your chances of being remembered. Remember, character is defined by actions. I encourage you to steadily pursue being remembered as a strong pillar, formed out of a solid foundation. Here's Paul's prayer from me to you found in Romans 1:9, "God knows how often I pray for you. Day and night I bring you and your needs in prayer to God, whom I serve with all my heart by spreading the Good News about his Son." God bless you, I love you and I believe in you. Despite the odds you will be remembered, believe it!

Love, Red

Dear you,

I encourage you to feed the circle of love in your life; for compassion goes a lot farther than some ten-cent gift, turned profit. Value the people in your life; take the time to show and receive love and strive to show your passion for compassion. I leave you with a great reference for your hip pocket toolbox; 1 John 4:9–11, "God showed how much He loved us by sending His one and only Son into the world so that we might have eternal life through Him. This is real love—not that we loved God, but that he loved us and sent his Son as a sacrifice to take away our sins. Dear friends, since God loved us that much, we surely ought to love each other." Passion, Compassion and Love…share some, build some. God bless you! Love y'all.

Love, Red

Dear you,

Set aside the self-serving attitude, get out of your comfort zone and be ready to step it up and out, rocking this thing called forward progress. I encourage you to stomp out, push out, drive out, whatever you gotta do to get that nasty ole negativity out of your life so that you can embrace, live, and emit positivity! Come on now, embrace the forward progress of positivity! Shout it out, "I'M READY to ROCK IT!" You can do it, Philippians 4:13 confirms it! God bless you! Now get after it!

Love, Red

Dear you,

Stop it; stop allowing self-doubt to stop you from rising from the ashes of defeat. Rise up, be victorious; be the inspiring leader you are destined to be! Your self-belief and confidence should be one of your strongest resources. Yes, terrible and hard things can happen, triggering those doubts, but you have the control and power to overcome; stop reliving the bad. Martha Beck put it this way, "Whatever terrible things may have happened to you, only one thing allows them to damage your core self, and that is continued belief in them." I encourage you to not complicate life, but appreciate it, and believe in yourself! After all, you are creating your life roadmap; the construction is continuous and the stops along the way influence the end destination. Spiritually, the power of Jesus's death, burial and resurrection is direct motivation of rising Victorious; it truly is inspiring to know that through Him we, indeed, have victory! He was beat down but not beaten. He was whipped but not destroyed. He was mocked but not silenced. He was crucified, but didn't forever die and is ever present and alive. He fights for you (Exodus 14:14)…so rise up and be victorious through Him. God bless you.

Love, Red

Dear you,

Empower and/or continue the establishment of unity, the power of many…operating as one, within your circles. Do not fear it, but revere it and consistently seek it. For in the pursuit of vision comes the mission followed by implementation through means of unified thought and reason. Vision begins as dreams, but will die if unity isn't alive. The power of many operating as one, leads to a victory won.

Love, Red

Dear you,

We've all had mentors, in some form, to help lead and guide us on this ride of life. In fact many of us have been one to others, introducing them to the right relationships at the right time. Why is it important? It builds trust. It shows that you value your team and want to strengthen each member by sharing your lessons learned and knowledge gained, which directly keeps the core of your team strong with the ability to rise to any occasion. John C. Maxwell once said, "The best way a mentor can prepare another leader is to expose him or her to other great people."; pair this with inspiration and encouragement and you will stimulate the proper growth and development required for success. I encourage each of us to learn, teach and lead at all levels, as we steadily stay on point! Spiritually, God is the ultimate Mentor. It is His Word that shapes us; your life is living proof to those you encounter that He is the game changer, that He is the life changing Mentor. Second Timothy 3:16 says, "All Scripture is inspired by God and is useful to teach us what is true and to make us realize what is wrong in our lives. It corrects us when we are wrong and teaches us to do what is right." God bless you and may your heavenly MENTOR shape how you mentor your team!

Love, Red

DEAR YOU

Dear you,

The revolution and revival for your life has begun; up to you to carry the torch in your own life, as you follow through in being the strongest you.

Love, Red

Dear you,

Don't be afraid to take that first step, second step, followed by continued steps…those steps of forward progress. Say, "I CAN AND I WILL"! I encourage you to keep your head up, shoulders back and confidently ride out this thing called life. You can do it. Stay solid and have a fantastic day. God bless you, and, if no one has told you today, I love you. Praying for you and yours. "God knows how often I pray for you. Day and night I bring you and your needs in prayer to God, whom I serve with all my heart by spreading the Good News about his Son." Romans 1:9.

Love, Red

Dear you,

Life driven by fear appears to be a lonely abyss; for fear inhibits your desire to fully live. Fear creates a downward spiral destined for failure, a life left empty. Stay inspired as you twist that throttle of life and ride it day and night fueled by a courageous drive to never give up the fight, the fight of achieving a full and successful life. Live life, live it well, love often and die right. God bless you.

Love, Red

Dear you,

From the heart; It's great to be an OVERCOMER! The year is almost over; if life and time continues for a couple more days, you can successfully say, "I MADE IT, I successfully overcame the year's ups and downs, the sadness and joy, life and death. I AM AN OVERCOMER!" Each day is a sign of completing yesterday, which is then filled with opportunities to live today, paving way for a new day. You see, life is short, we are but a mere breath away from death, but do not fear, for you are an OVERCOMER! I am reminded, followed by encouraged, of the sadness of Christ's death turned to joy in His resurrection; for, it's an instant reminder that, through Him, I am an OVERCOMER. John 16 is a solid passage on sadness turning to joy and the ultimate example of overcoming the world. You, yes you, are not alone. The joy in His resurrection left you with the Holy Spirit, otherwise known as the Comforter. Read it…check it out. I leave you with verse 33 as encouragement to keep on keeping on in living today while paving the way for new days. "I have told you all this so that you may have peace in me. Here on earth you will have many trials and sorrows. But take heart, because I have overcome the world."-John 16:33. So end the year with joy and bring in the new as a strong OVERCOMER! As Pastor Kevin McGlamery, of Life Church Huntsville, says, "We are better together!" You are not alone.

Love, Red

Dear you,

People tend to forget that a Leader with the vision has a tough job; for it is the Leader who is held accountable in following the vision at a deeper level than the team. Hence, Leaders need the teams to support them in order to fulfill the vision. As the Leader leads by example, the team should follow suit. I encourage you, as a Leader, to embrace the vision put in motion and influence your team by actions not words, which will directly allow room for growth and true mentoring. I encourage you, as members of the team, to support your Leader's vision, for they have a tough job. Reminds me, with a spiritual twist, of what Dallas Willard once said, "If you have a group of people come together around a vision for real discipleship, people who are committed to grow, committed to change, committed to learn, then a spiritual assessment tool can work." This concept applies to all rides of life; come together as a team, commit to grow, commit to change and learn! It's up to you to influence your team. God bless you and stay encouraged, as you keep on keeping on with implementing your vision. Change is inevitable; it's what you do with the change that affects the future.

Love, Red

Dear you,

One of the worst things you can do to someone is to lie to them. For once you lie it is almost impossible to ever regain the level of trust you once had; it is as if a part of you has died when you lie. Michel de Montaigne once said, "I do myself a greater injury in lying than I do him of whom I tell a lie." Meaning that when you lie you compromise you, damaging your values and reputation. I encourage each of us to be open to honest criticism, rather than slippery flattery founded on lies. "In the end, people appreciate honest criticism far more than flattery" (Proverbs 28:23). God bless you!

Love, Red

Dear you,

Opportunities surround you every day; opportunities to help another, as well as work on being a better you. Up to you to seize the moments and influence the momentum of life's pendulum. The essence of time is priceless.

Love, Red

Dear you,

Emotions are in all of us, even if we are exercising the emotions needed to not respond in an emotional manner. The input you allow will directly, as well as indirectly, influence your emotional output. You have free will to stay strong; exercise discernment and wisdom in the will you decide to implement. It takes an internal understanding in knowing who you are and what you want if you want the discernment in your wisdom to show. Knowledge grows wisdom and drives the creation of discerning loyalty. I am praying for God's favor upon your wisdom and growth in discerning understanding. Hit up Romans 1:9. God is here. God bless you.

Love, Red

DEAR YOU

Dear you,

The struggles of life are real, for you and I live them daily, but being humble and meek doesn't mean weak. Being humble, meek, and the first to show kindness, comes with mature wisdom; shows your true inner strength, a constant in my life. Despite the struggle there is Hope. You might say, "Red, what gives you the ability to be strong, yet meek and humble?" My reply is wisdom, knowledge, loyalty, integrity and the right mentors; with God, now, being my number 1 mentor. War in life happens and comes in many different forms. Proverbs 24:5–6 (NLT) says, "The wise are mightier than the strong, and those with knowledge grow stronger and stronger. So don't go to war without wise guidance; victory depends on having many advisers." I pray for you today and for God's favor to shine upon you and yours; allow your eyes to be opened to the truth of Hope, to include the ability to be meek, humble and the first to extend the olive branch. Without hope we have already lost the battle. The strength of one is better than none; show your Brother and Sister the way. God bless you. I love you and know that the best is yet to come.

Love, Red

Dear you,

"The two most important days in your life are the day you are born and the day you find out why" (Mark Twain). Finding out why can take a lifetime; enjoy the ride, but I encourage you, as you continue the journey, to stay purpose driven. God bless you and yours. Stay solid.

Love, Red

Dear you,

Let your character be the character another seeks after. Keep in mind that your patience, temper, strength, those things that comprise your character will, inevitably, be tested. Stay in control, stay character driven; driven to a selfless ride of life. Amy Hendren McGlamery, from Life Church Huntsville, said, "We emit what we absorb!" I encourage each of us to endure the ride, seek out ways to improve our character and let truth reside so that our reflection emits what's inside. Truth can only be imitated before the truth is found out. God bless you, as you get after it today!

Love, Red

Dear you,

Today is your day! Do not let the power of persuasion rule your life, consistently live and pursue the truth. Yes, this means that sometimes you will stand alone, but sometimes you will find yourself surrounded by fellow lions standing at the ready. Reminds me of a Tibetan Proverb which says, "It's better to live for one day as a lion than for one thousand years as a sheep." So shout it out, "Today is my day, to stand on solid ground and reach new heights! I will not let the madness of life fill my mind or soul, but rather will roll with determination of reaching all things great in my life!" You can do it; I believe in you, make that vision come to life! After seeking I found my truth in John 3:16 and live daily to reflect all that I am in Him. God bless you and may you have a solid day!

Love, Red

Dear you,

Don't let your focus on tomorrow hinder you living today. For it is in today that you might just see the vision for a stronger tomorrow; without a vision you have no mission. Kevin McGlamery, from Life Church Huntsville, said "You have to see it before you see it." Meaning, before you see it you must envision it, develop it and, then, work toward implementing it. I encourage you to open your eyes, physically and spiritually, in your pursuit of becoming a better you. John 3:30 says, "He must increase, but I must decrease." Praying for God's favor upon your week and may He show you something new. God bless you.

Love, Red

Dear you,

Relationships should be unified with purpose to impact influence; inherent to influence is the ability to be the example. So why do many relationships and teams start off strong, but tend to fall apart? Human pride and lack of humble attitudes; we live in a selfish and prideful world full of people wanting to prove they are the greatest, even if they destroy others to reach the top. First Corinthians 10:12, followed by a solid Proverb found in 16:18 says, "If you think you are standing strong, be careful not to fall. Pride goes before destruction, and haughtiness before a fall!" I encourage you to remember that your attitude and actions must be right in order to bring about and/or influence strategic change within your team. We should stay humble and cease the grumble. God bless you and yours!

Love, Red

Dear you,

Let's have a quick heart to heart; solid leadership requires compassion. Many on your team or in your circle of life will be experiencing their first year of holidays without a loved one. Many circumstances surround this; however, a dominant reason is that loss of life has occurred, leaving them feeling empty, alone and even angry. I get it, loss, it's a part of life, but having compassion for others directly helps them get through the process. I, myself, know this feeling and have experienced the aforementioned emotions, as well as have experienced the internal reward of being there for another. I encourage you, as a leader, to inspire others, be compassionate and make others aware that they are not alone. This emotional side of leadership requires extending a piece of your heart to them; you won't regret it. Remember, just because someone is smiling on the outside, you never know what's going on inside. "So encourage each other and build each other up, just as you are already doing" (1 Thessalonians 5:11). God bless you!

Love, Red

Dear you,

"WE" must NEVER give up on Unity, Hope, or Overcoming negativity. Each day we all face something, both good and bad. Bad things happen…it's a fact of life. How we deal with them speaks on our faith in God. Even through the dark and treacherous times of our life God is here with arms wide open full of grace, mercy, forgiveness and salvation. "WE" must know that it is us that leave Him not He who leaves us. We must stay encouraged, steadily encouraging one another in order to effectively witness.

Love, Red

Dear you,

Know that being prayed up strong in the Spirit is key to our life. In fact, prayer is a key tool to have in our spiritual toolbox. In Habakkuk 3 we have a great example of this tool. As you read it, focus on verses 18–19. Why? Because you will read about the bad, dark and treacherous times, but because of Habakkuk's faith he overcame as read in 18–19. How? Through his faith…that's how. So as "WE" as a community travel through these times we proudly keep this in our hip pocket: "Through my bad, dark and treacherous moments I will pull out my tool of prayer and unconditionally rejoice in the Lord!"

Love, Red

Dear you,

Know that as His servants we must show that we are strong in the Lord. Why? This shows the strength of giving our life to Christ. As we all work through this process, "WE" must stay vigilant in our fight as God's servants. The Sovereign Lord is "OUR" Strength!" "WE" must stay unified by being true to God. We need not let another human or situation steal our joy. Remember the ones we are here for look to us for consistency in our actions to match our speech. I encourage us all to seek the guidance of the Holy Spirit to go before us, setting our day. Unity is shown in our daily lives not just talked about. In 1 John 3:18 (NLT) it say…let's not merely say that we love each other; let us show the truth by our actions.

Love, Red

Dear you,

Despite the many obstacles and the bad things that happen in this world, "WE "must maintain hope through Unity that those we encounter will see Jesus through us and our ride of life…leading some along our ride to join us in the pursuit of God's straight and narrow. "WE" insert ourselves into the world in order to show it ours. During these difficult times it is imperative for us to stay unified and strong to encourage one another as a means of protection, both physically and spiritually. This in turn allows us to maintain who we are when the world comes to us for shelter, prayers, help and advice. Unity among us keeps God in it as referenced in Matthew 18:20 (NLT), "For where two or three gather together as my followers, I am there among them." God bless you join us in consistent prayer for the Holy Spirit to guide "Our Ride."

Love, Red

Dear you,

Attitudes and actions are contagious, and its worthy to mention, we each are carriers of multiple strands. I would rather be infected with positivity than well and full from negativity. Tom Stoppard once said, "A healthy attitude is contagious but don't wait to catch it from others. Be a carrier!" I encourage you to be healthy, full of positivity; spread the disease so others can catch it! The rewards are far greater than staying sick with negativity. Spiritually, Psalm 103:1 is a solid reference to which strand you should emit to the world around you. "Let all that I am praise the Lord; with my whole heart, I will praise His Holy name." Share the message of hope and positivity; a healthy attitude is contagious, so pass it on. Praying for God's favor upon your day and for Him to restore your attitude back to a healthy state. God bless you!

Love, Red

DEAR YOU

Dear you,

Take the time to thank the one who created it all, God. I encourage each of us to keep teaching, sharing and displaying the characteristics of thankfulness in our lives; for we have much to be thankful for on a daily basis, with life being one at the top. I leave you with a solid reference found in Colossians 3:16 which reads, "Let the message about Christ, in all its richness, fill your lives. Teach and counsel each other with all the wisdom He gives. Sing psalms and hymns and spiritual songs to God with thankful hearts." God bless you and yours on this wonderful day!

Love, Red

Dear you,

Take the time to truly know those within your circle. Getting to know the truth behind a smile or frown is far more important than simply knowing their name. You see, sometimes the smile is simply hiding an internal frown, an internal pain not externally seen. I encourage each of us to truly demonstrate and experience the fullness of love, which goes deeper than just a four letter word. God bless you.

Love, Red

Dear you,

Staying strong is hard, but must be done when walking it out. Facing good and bad is inevitable, we all have and will to come, but, yes, at times, it's hard physically and mentally to see the light at the end of the tunnel, to see God's hands in the midst of our earthly trials and for us to wrap our minds on the "why." However, stand fast and trust that He is working things in your favor. Be reminded of Isaiah 55:8 which says, ""My thoughts are nothing like your thoughts," says the Lord. And my ways are far beyond anything you could imagine." I encourage each of us to know that our God is stronger than our problems and that His ways have a solid purpose. As for me and my family we will keep fighting the fight for His will to prevail. Will you do the same in your life? We are overcomers. God bless you.

Love, Red

Dear you,

What a wonderful morning it is, so get out there and take advantage of all the wonderful things right in front of you! With each breath you take, take value in how wonderful that in itself truly is. It means another day to right your wrongs, another day to spend with family, another day to share the love of Jesus, another day to succeed where you failed yesterday, another day to smile in the face of life's adversities; for you have been blessed with another day to pave the way; make it count. God bless you!

Love, Red

Dear you,

Be remembered as honorable, rather than dishonorable; be remembered as truthful, rather than a liar; be remembered as selfless, rather than selfish; be remembered as compassionate, rather than hateful; be remembered as one with convictions, rather than indecisive; be remembered as one of God's, rather than a lost soul; BE REMEMBERED. First Peter 2:15 says, "It is God's will that your honorable lives should silence those ignorant people who make foolish accusations against you." Every action causes a reaction and stamps into a permanent memory. Be remembered for a solid reputation, rather than forgotten with a broken legacy. God bless you!

Love, Red

Dear you,

With all the mania, sadness, ignorance, pain, etc....ongoing in our country, maybe even in your own personal life, it is so imperative to pray. Life influences each of us differently, because each of us are emotionally and spiritually driven in different ways. However, we have been equipped with the power of prayer and prayer in action leads to reactions. One day all the mania and pain of this nasty ole earth will be over; the problem is that we do not know when that time will be. Until then, we should pray each and every day for ourselves and others. Bottom line is that you can only control yourself, but can pray for others. Remember it's not the choice, but the consequence of that choice you are left to deal with. First Timothy 2:1 says, "I urge you, first of all, to pray for all people. Ask God to help them; intercede on their behalf, and give thanks for them." Stay encouraged, keep praying for yourself and others and stay focused on becoming a better you. God bless you!

Love, Red

Dear you,

Reality can be altered; it takes vision and self-leadership to change circumstances. In life we all have a current reality; it's up to us to define it, accept it or change it. Your dreams, your destiny, can end up becoming an adventurous versus lifeless reality. Warren Bennis once said, "Leadership is the capacity to translate vision into reality." I encourage you to exercise wisdom, self-lead, keep your head up and shoulders back, as you keep pushing toward making your reality the best in order to influence the rest. I leave you with James 1:5a, "If you need wisdom, ask our generous God, and he will give it to you..." God bless you!

Love, Red

Dear you,

I'm reminded how grateful I am for the little things, such as bread and sandwich spread. For without these two things it makes eating a sandwich doable, but messy, dry or even repulsive. Take time to notice the little things and take note to how they impact the big things in your life. In regards to life we each have friends, we each have enemies; we each have people for us, as well as those set out against us. You see, enemies are small things in regards to the big life picture. Without them we might just get too comfortable, while with them we steadily stay the course, always prepared to overcome. Yes, it gets messy, but my God enables me to handle the messy and keeps me hands clean. Spiritually, I'm reminded that we should be thankful for the little things, such as a verse or prayer. For without these two things life is doable, but with them our God life stays on point. For example, Psalms 3 talks about enemies and even includes a prayer to God. Victory is found in even the smallest things, so cherish all things in your life; even the messy. God bless you!

Love, Red

DEAR YOU

Dear you,

Life happens. Take a hard look at your life, take a deep breath and begin today with forgiving yourself. Forgiveness is not something earned, it is a gift; to not only those you forgive, but an internal peace gift to you. Let today be a breath of fresh air and a fresh start to life, beginning with forgiveness; yesterday is gone, so kick start your today. No matter the hurt you have experienced, or the hurt you are experiencing, you have the power of forgiveness, the gift of His grace, His Mercy and ultimately His forgiveness. How? Through His death, an act of love for you. Second Corinthians 5:17 (NLT) says, "This means that anyone who belongs to Christ has become a new person. The old life is gone; a new life has begun!" I encourage you to forgive, smile and get your new life on and live it to the fullest, for life is short. God bless you!

Love, Red

Dear you,

If you want the world to change you have to speak up and lead by example. If you do nothing, nothing changes; leaving you with no room to complain. Actions are louder than words and words without action are mere fiction until brought to life through action. "So, my dear brothers and sisters, be strong and immovable. Always work enthusiastically for the Lord, for you know that nothing you do for the Lord is ever useless" (1 Corinthians 15:58). Stay the course, make the needed changes. Pray for me as I pray for you. God bless you!

Love, Red

Dear you,

Let's face some truth, someone you know or someone reading this is facing some type of uncertainty, which tends to lead to despair, fear, anger and/or a feeling of nothing matters, not even them. Life legacy is forever, moments of despair are mere moments of time; don't let these moments stop you from pulling yourself up or from reaching out to God and the people surrounding you for help. You are an overcomer; STAND STRONG! If it's you, I want you to know that you matter, you are important and you are cherished. Yes, sometimes it is hard to be brave, it is hard to keep on, it is hard to be patient, but we have an awesome life manual, the Bible, to turn to. Psalm 27:14 says, "Wait patiently for the Lord. Be brave and courageous. Yes, wait patiently for the Lord." Overcome uncertainty through Him, for He calls you an Overcomer. I leave you with 1 John 5:4 "For everyone who has been born of God overcomes the world. And this is the victory that has overcome the world—our faith." God bless you today!

Love, Red

Dear you,

Put a smile on that face and experience a day like never before, achieve what you have been working so hard toward and minimize the complexities in life by maximizing the realization of its simplicity! Joy, happiness, contentment all come from within. So enjoy the things, people and circumstances in your life; for they are signs that you are indeed alive! Live a life of faith, you live a life of simplicity; for when we believe in Him we live life in the essence of simplicity. As you smile, enjoy life, accomplish life, and remember, He is not the author nor creator of confusion, but the God of inexplicable peace. As Paul said in 2 Thessalonians 3:16, "Now may the Lord of peace Himself give you His peace at all times and in every situation. The Lord be with you all." YES INDEED! Live life, live it well and die right. God bless you.

Love, Red

Dear you,

Preparation is wise, and key, to accomplishing just about anything. This morning, while taking in the movement of nature with some coffee, I saw birds picking at seeds that have fallen from trees, I saw squirrels gathering up nuts, and saw some chipmunks chasing each other with packed cheeks. The intriguing and amazing thing is realizing that all of their movement shows the wisdom in nature and how smart creatures are by preparing for the change of seasons. They instinctively know to prepare and have been programmed with the wisdom and knowledge to do so. We can learn a lot from nature. Seasons change in our lives, which is why we must prepare on a daily basis for the storms, the shifts in climates and then follow through with change by exhibiting the wisdom to be prepared. Wisdom and knowledge saves lives, make them part of your natural instincts. Proverbs 24:5 says, "The wise are mightier than the strong, and those with knowledge grow stronger and stronger." God bless you.

Love, Red

Dear you,

Keep pressing forward, as you rise victorious against every obstacle; triumph in believing that you have already overcome those objectives yet to be negotiated. The power of self-belief is an enabler for victory.

Love, Red

Dear you,

Fulfilling Obligations. We all face some type of obligation. It is integrity and a choice to fulfill what you have obligated yourself to do. Whether it be an event, a meeting, etc.…it is a requirement to fulfill; fulfilling obligations speaks to who you are and shows what your personal character is truly made of. We are under no obligation to sin (Romans 8:12), but rather are obligated to Him, especially seeing as has how He has obligated no condemnation to us, His followers. Romans 8:1–2 says, "So now there is no condemnation for those who belong to Christ Jesus. And because you belong to Him, the power of the life-giving Spirit has freed you from the power of sin that leads to death." I encourage you to fulfill your obligations, first to Him, and in life; for your character fuels your legacy. He has set you free in the Spirit; fulfill your obligations. God bless you.

Love, Red

DEAR YOU

Dear you,

Deep roots stand fast through the storms, shallow roots uproot and deteriorate. You mustn't let circumstances determine your joy or destroy your roots. Storms and trials of life, such as divorce, custody battles, finances, health, loss of job, relationships, etc...., will come against you; how you stand strong shows your internal strength to external enemies. It is during these storms that your character is made stronger, your spirit is strengthened by the Spirit and your roots, which is up to you, will either stay rooted or become uprooted. I encourage you to stay rooted, full of joy, and know that no mistake, nor storm, changes God's plan for your life. He enables your roots to become unmovable, unbreakable and unshakable. Be moved by Him not by storms exposing shallow roots. Colossians 2:6–7 says, "And now, just as you accepted Christ Jesus as your Lord, you must continue to follow Him. Let your roots grow down into Him, and let your lives be built on Him. Then your faith will grow strong in the truth you were taught, and you will overflow with thankfulness." God bless you as you get after life today. Be strengthened not weakened.

Love, Red

Dear you,

Honesty is a dwindling trait and emotions can cloud your vision; be mindful that, sometimes, you have to emotionally remove yourself so that you can identify the truths in order to process the situation. A path forward with honesty will rise above emotion based journeys; the similarity is that an end destination will be reached, how you get there is reliant on you and your actions. When you don't feel able…He makes you able. When you feel tired…He keeps you going. When you feel like nobody loves you…He loves you unconditionally. When you get confused and don't understand…He gives you discernment and directs you. When you say I just can't do it… He says you can do all things through Him. He is the essence of HOPE and has a worthy legacy filled with truth, love, honesty, wisdom and so much more. "He" is God. Let us stay encouraged to seek out discernment, wisdom and knowledge; even when we don't understand. Romans 11:33 says, "Oh, how great are God's riches and wisdom and knowledge! How impossible it is for us to understand his decisions and his ways!" God bless you!

Love, Red

Dear you,

Limitations Exceeded. Don't limit yourself, go after your dreams; exceed your limitations. Don't just think about it go and get after it! Many sit idle, getting nowhere, because they fail to ask or fail to pursue. Success comes with proactive asking and/or proactive movement, not just waiting; ask God and, if it be in His Will for you, it shall be. Luke 11:9–10 says, "And so I tell you, keep on asking, and you will receive what you ask for. Keep on seeking, and you will find. Keep on knocking, and the door will be opened to you. For everyone who asks, receives. Everyone who seeks, finds. And to everyone who knocks, the door will be opened." Let your dreams inspire your drive. God bless you and yours today!

Love, Red

DEAR YOU

Dear you,

Unity strengthens, as obstacles of life and diversity are overcome. Unity of hope, unity of encouragement, unity in totality; we may say impossible, but put God in the middle of the word and He says, "I'm Possible not impossible." Unity and diversity brings about an atmosphere of success, as core competencies are aligned in support of synergy. First Corinthians 12:12–31 is a great point of reference.

Love, Red

Dear you,

Chains. Chains are tools of restraint. Some chains are self-imposed, some are wrongfully imposed; however, whatever chains have you bound, you can break them in the name of Jesus. Life events bring along those mental and/or spiritual chains, leaving scars. Scars and chains in your life are being broken and repaired; watch God work and overcome in your life, you're free. We may know what happened and how it happened, but left with never knowing why it happened, and that's okay. I encourage you to stay reminded that, in the midst of everything, you are never bound left alone; for God is always with you. Be set free in the name of Jesus. "Therefore if the Son makes you free, you shall be free indeed" (John 8:36). God bless you!

Love, Red

Dear you,

Relationships are unified and/or bound together through purpose; when you lead from the front you have the opportunity to improve and solidify these relationships. Don't complicate life, appreciate it. Look at today as the first day of the rest of your life and be that Leader to model after; remember, when you are at your best you influence the rest. Yes, we live in a selfish and prideful world full of people wanting to prove they are the greatest in many aspects, even if they have to destroy others to reach the top. However, pride eventually destroys them, along with their relationships. A solid Proverb found in 16:18 says, "Pride goes before destruction, and haughtiness before a fall." Be encouraged to remain humble, as you lead from the font. None of us can change the past, but we can cherish the here and now, being the best we can be. What will be your legacy say about how you impacted the relationships in your life? God bless you.

Love, Red

Dear you,

Words. Words spoken can offer a token of appreciation or leave someone broken. As a leader, allow your words to be filled with wisdom, truth, compassion and inspiration. The atmosphere we foster starts with our words. "Wise words bring many benefits, and hard work brings rewards" (Proverbs 12:14). I encourage you, foster a positive atmosphere, full of synergy, by carefully choosing your words; you can't take them back. I leave you with Proverbs 12:25, which says, "Worry weighs a person down; an encouraging word cheers a person up." God bless you.

Love, Red

DEAR YOU

Dear you,

Suffering is inevitable in life…it's simply part of the ride; just make sure you are suffering for the right reasons and the right cause. First Peter 4:12–19 is a solid passage. Pay attention to verse 19, "So if you are suffering in a manner that pleases God, keep on doing what is right, and trust your lives to the God who created you, for he will never fail you." The point is that standing for God, your family, your children, your Brothers and Sisters will, at times, cause suffering, but WE mustn't waiver on truth or God. Rise up for RIGHT! God bless you.

Love, Red

Dear you,

Every road taken has led to today. The past, good or bad, is a stepping stone for today. We all have room for improvement; We all have burdens; and We all have been lost and wandering on lost roads leading nowhere. The core thing we all have in common is that nothing that you or I have done, even the unspeakable things, can overcome the power of His blood.

Love, Red

Dear you,

Inheritance. Each day brings opportunities to inherit glory as you develop your legacy. Second and third order effects of your decisions need to be considered, for it's those effects that create the consequences you are left to process and are the direct input to what your legacy will be. A solid Proverb found in 3:35 says, "The wise shall inherit glory, but shame shall be the legacy of fools." Stay encouraged, seek wisdom and inherit glory; let no shame fall on your name. Life's moments can be duplicated, but not relived; make each one important, memorable and one that supports a solid legacy. God bless you!

Love, Red

Dear you,

Each of us must grow and thrive in the face of challenges. Let it be about "WE" not "ME." "WE" will bounce back from adversity, while building the core competencies that enable mental and physical toughness, optimal performance, strong leadership, and goal achievement; sound traits of Brotherhood and Sisterhood. "WE" will counter negative thoughts with positive reactions, which in turn creates positive rotation of the wheel to which "WE" belong. You MUST believe it, receive and declare it. Now get out there and implement it; positive movement within your wheel is in your grasp, make it GREAT! First Peter 4:7–11 is a great passage to show that "WE" have been enabled through HIM to succeed. Verse 10 says, "God has given each of you a gift from His great variety of spiritual gifts. Use them well to serve one another." Praying for forward progress in all aspects of our lives. Be blessed today.

Love, Red

DEAR YOU

Dear you,

Forward progress is just that…forward progress. Imagine a door in front of you, and on the other side of the door is your objective. If you move backward the door gets smaller and smaller; however, if you progress forward you get closer and closer to negotiating the door and achieving your objective. It is self-discipline, a commitment that enables you to persevere, moving forward. In life we face many doors and many objectives. As a leader it is up to you to maintain the dedication to lead yourself and, at times, your team through the doors with forward momentum to overcome each and every objective life throws your way. A defining factor is your inner strength and how well defined your level of commitment truly is. Whatever it is you are facing…you…yes you, have been enabled with the courage and strength to persevere. Spiritually, when you add God to your life that courage and strength multiplies. Joshua 1:9 is just one of over 50+ scriptures confirming this truth; it says, "This is my command—be strong and courageous! Do not be afraid or discouraged. For the Lord your God is with you wherever you go." Stay encouraged and keep moving forward! God bless you!

Love, Red

Dear you,

Preventative maintenance directly contributes to the life cycle of your ride, which is why you check the tire pressure, oil pressure, etc.… It helps reduce the time between failures. Guess what? Leadership skills and traits also require preventative maintenance; self-examination is key to identifying points of failure and instituting corrective action to stay on course leads to success. The standards you set for yourself trickle down to the standards and quality of your team. Ray Kroc said, "The quality of a leader is reflected in the standards they set for themselves." Spiritually, we must update our spiritual log book to ensure our spiritual ride is in balance. If you have a shake or wobble give it over to God; for where you are shakable, He is unshakable. First Peter 5:7 says, "Give all your worries and cares to God, for He cares about you." As you get after it today, institute corrective actions where necessary in all aspects of your life. God bless you.

Love, Red

Dear you,

Life is limitless, when you try; life is limitless, when you believe in yourself. Do not be a traitor or the creator of doubt to yourself, but rather the author of success that writes the story of a fearless life lived limitless. Shakespeare once said, "Our doubts are traitors, and make us lose the good we oft might win, by fearing to attempt." So be creative and confident in whatever it is you set out to attempt, believe in yourself and keep your head held up. Spiritually, with Christ, life is indeed limitless. I leave you with Philippians 4:13 for your hip pocket, "For I can do ALL THINGS through Christ, who gives me strength."

Love, Red

DEAR YOU

Dear you,

Impact of Overflow. Think about a glass of water, it can be full to the rim, but until it overflows it has no true impact on its surroundings; it is the overflow that has the greatest impact, creating a series of reactions and actions. Now relate this concept to leadership. A leader can be busting at the seams with knowledge, but if they do not allow it to overflow to their team then their impacts will be minimal. However, if they allow their knowledge to overflow in ways of teaching, sharing and mentoring then they will have positive impacts while directly generating a path to success. Spiritually, one can be so full of Jesus, but until they allow their love and relationship to overflow they will have minimal impacts; it is the overflow of that relationship that shows another the way. I encourage you to allow your knowledge to overflow as you build a stronger team and leave you with a prayer found in Romans 15:13. "I pray that God, the source of hope, will fill you completely with joy and peace because you trust in him. Then you will overflow with confident hope through the power of the Holy Spirit." God bless you and may your week be super fantastic!

Love, Red

Dear you,

Life shouldn't be all about what you get, but rather in part what you give. Material things, titles, etc.…matter not when you die, but your legacy as a person does; Matthew 6:19–21 is a great point of reference. Verse 21 says, "Wherever your treasure is, there the desires of your heart will also be." In the words of Winston Churchill, "We make a living by what we get, but we make a LIFE by what we give." I encourage you, make a life to remember and to help show another the way. Remember, time is one of the most precious gifts; think about it. God bless you and have a fantastic weekend!

Love, Red

Dear you,

Why even try? Try what? Being a friend, being a Brother or Sister, being a confidant, being an ally, simply being a being; because it seems when we try we are let down and begin to slowly, internally, die. Why try? Because you are a human BEING, so being is innate… it comes natural to try. Never stop giving it a try until the day you die. Know that you aren't able to make everyone happy. Be a being, be real and do your best to be at your best. DON'T GIVE UP! I believe in you and, yes, greater things are to be, so be a BEING!

Love, Red

Dear you,

Leaders are looked at to encourage, inspire, motivate and strengthen the morale of the team; it costs nothing to simply say, "Thank you, keep up the good work!" "If your actions inspire others to dream more, learn more, do more and become more, you are a leader" (John Quincy Adams). Spiritually, continue to look to God as the ultimate example of what a leader is and stay encouraged to consistently improve your best as you influence the rest. Second Timothy 2:15 says, "Do your best to present yourself to God as one approved, a worker who has no need to be ashamed, rightly handling the word of truth." God bless you.

Love, Red

Dear you,

Bitterness is destructive; counterproductive to success. You see, bitterness is a result of some form of a letdown, which has destroyed many relationships along the way. This is why it's imperative for you, as a leader, to emotionally connect with those on your team in order to prevent the nasty contagious thing called bitterness from spreading. Why must you get in front of it to prevent it? Well, when troubles hit and bitterness sets in, the leader is, generally, the one targeted. I encourage you to be inspired to do your part in leading from the front by not letting bitterness set into your life. For me, I am reminded of what Harry Emerson Fosdick said, "Bitterness imprisons life; love releases it." Spiritually, I leave you with Ephesians 4:31a, "Get rid of all bitterness, rage, anger, harsh words, and slander…" Stay strong as you steadily overcome. God bless you!

Love, Red

Dear you,

Fleas, they become a problem if not treated. You have to isolate the location and treat the area. If there is an infestation you have to dip the entire animal or cover it entirely with the proper medicine. Until fixed, the animal is miserable and inflicts self-damage by the intense scratching. Fleas symbolize the problems in our lives; find the fleas, then scratch. If you don't fix the problems in your life you end up being miserable and the self-damage can become irreversible. I encourage you to realize that God is the #1 medicine; don't be afraid to be dipped, filled and covered by His love. Isolate the problems and eradicate the fleas. God bless you!

Love, Red

Dear you,

The Butterfly. They were once a lowly caterpillar, scooting along the earth, fighting for their spot to secure their transformation. They grow, change and morph, as they transform into a magnificent and beautiful butterfly. No longer scooting along the earth, barely getting by, but soaring through the air! Their time in the cocoon represents your past. Do not let the failures of your past keep defining who you are today, but rather show the world how spectacular you have become! Fear not as you transform into a new creation…go ahead… the transformation is spot on and abundantly rewarding! Take this day head-on! Achieve every objective, embrace each new opportunity and be the shining example of happy! Live life, life it well and die right. God bless you and I pray for God's favor to be upon your life.

Love, Red

Dear you,

The race of life is much stronger when the following three Proverbs are implemented, they lead to a stronger you. (1) Better to be poor and honest than to be dishonest and a fool. (2) Enthusiasm without knowledge is no good; haste makes mistakes. (3) People ruin their lives by their own foolishness and then are angry at the Lord" (Proverbs 19:1–3). The blame game is a shame, especially when one tries to blame God; one must own their faults, after all they made their choices. God desires good for you; He doesn't set you up to fail. Be encouraged to finish the race with patience and integrity, built in part on solid knowledge. Live life, live it well and die right. God bless you!

Love, Red

Dear you,

You have a purpose and are a valued player, even when you feel as if there is no hope. Do NOT let hopelessness become a weakness; weakness destroys greatness. Strength in life leadership is not simply situation driven; it is something consistently demonstrated. Focus on the positives and prevent negatives from clouding your greatness; yes, it takes endurance…the will to never give up. You can do it; I believe in you! Be encouraged to maintain the commitment to persevere and you will succeed. Spiritually, Romans 5:1–5 is solid motivation! Verse 4 says, "And endurance develops strength of character, and character strengthens our confident hope of salvation." God bless you!

Love, Red

Dear you,

Your ride of life is only ordinary if you allow it. It is what it is, right? Wrong. You, yes you, have the power to drive the change, improve and make a difference, as you accomplish that next milestone. You have been empowered to live more than an just an ordinary life, you deserve spectacular; so get after it! Solid Leadership will uplift, encourage and motivate; it takes genuine effort, but with the effort comes the domino effect of change. Be encouraged to exercise strength in being the change and Leader needed. After all, you're only as good as you will be today; yesterday is gone and tomorrow may not come. Will your legacy be one to model? "Let us consider how to stir up one another to love and good works, not neglecting to meet together, as is the habit of some, but encouraging one another, and all the more as you see the Day drawing near" (Hebrews 10:24–25). God bless you!

Love, Red

Dear you,

Words can be a deadly trap; don't become your worst enemy. Be mindful and careful of what you allow to proceed from your mouth; build up versus tear down. As a Leader, it's up to you to demonstrate self-control, be self-aware and cognizant that your speech influences success. I leave you with Proverbs 12:13–14. "The wicked are trapped by their own words, but the Godly escape such trouble." NOTE verse 14: "Wise words bring many benefits, and hard work brings rewards." Be encouraged to lead from the front and build the bench by setting the proper example. God bless you and may you have a super fantastic week!

Love, Red

DEAR YOU

Dear you,

Getting through the storm. Are you going through a storm? Maybe you just weathered a storm. The point is that you will inevitably face storms throughout life. How you choose to handle it, and lead others through it, speaks to who you are as a person, as well as a Leader. Through experience, you recognize the need to change course or to carry on. The choice is one only you can make, but remember the choice is not the end; consequences follow. Consequences of your choice are what you are left to weather. I encourage you to always do due diligence in projecting the second and third order effects of your choices to minimize risk, as you mitigate each consequence. As a follower of Christ you are not alone, there are over twenty-eight biblical references on weathering storms. His power is real and evident; He is your stronghold and refuge through the storms. "The Lord is good, a strong refuge when trouble comes. He is close to those who trust in him" (Nahum 1:7). I leave you with a prayer. "Dear Jesus, please watch over each and every one and guide them through the storms, protecting them along the way." God bless you!

Love, Red

Dear you,

The power of touch. From the time you wake up to the time you go to sleep you touch many things. It is one of the senses that provides physical confirmation to the mind that there is some tangible object present; even when you can't see it, smell it or hear it the power of touch makes it real. Your life, your character, who you are touches the hearts and lives of many; meaning that the value of your physical presence impacts the senses of your peers. As a Leader, the power of your touch impacts. How it impacts is reliant on your reality based on the perceptions of others, which are powered by how well you project your touch; your character creates the projection. Spiritually, God's touch is made real by touching the tangible book, the Bible. Hebrews 4:12 says, "For the word of God is alive and powerful. It is sharper than the sharpest two-edged sword, cutting between soul and spirit, between joint and marrow. It exposes our innermost thoughts and desires." Be encouraged by the power of touch and allow the Word of God to touch you and form your character. Then, as a Leader, you will be empowered with an effective touch on the things you, daily, touch. God bless you.

Love, Red

Dear you,

Found what you're looking for? If not, don't give up on your pursuit of success. Be committed and fully present in whatever situation you are in if you desire to overcome, succeed and win; be present, be active and bring imagination to life. As a Leader you know that your actions are being modeled after; make them actions of success not a mess. Keep the course, ask questions, steadily pursue and eventually the doors will be opened to you. "Keep on asking, and you will receive what you ask for. Keep on seeking, and you will find. Keep on knocking, and the door will be opened to you." Matthew 7:7. God bless you. Stay strong for the roads are long.

Love, Red

DEAR YOU

Dear you,

Be results driven. Your level of commitment and dedication is a driving factor; dedication throughout the good and bad. Remember, your level of commitment contributes to who you are and the legacy you are creating. As a follower of Christ, we stay committed because we know that our God of grace strengthens and guides us. Isaiah 41:10 says, "Don't be afraid, for I am with you. Don't be discouraged, for I am your God. I will strengthen you and help you. I will hold you up with my victorious right hand!" So be results driven; for your legacy depends on how well you drive. Stay solid and keep it throttled on the narrow. See you soon.

Love, Red

Dear you,

Let each one of us value God, our family and each other; for we all are one breath away from death. Each one of us makes an impact on another; yes you do. When we fail to share the love of Jesus we found, have and live we are directly leaving that Brother or Sister behind; share the gift. Personally, I don't want to see any of you left behind; I want to spend eternity with you. Romans 5:8 says, "But God showed his great love for us by sending Christ to die for us while we were still sinners." We aren't sinless, but strive to sin less. God bless you.

Love, Red

Dear you,

Leadership starts with self-leadership and reveals self-confidence. When we know ourselves and respect the similarities and differences we each bring to the table we are indeed contributing to the bigger picture. I encourage you to embody and cultivate inner strength. Personal leadership strikes deep, leaving a lasting impact. Second Timothy 1:7 says, "For God has not given us a spirit of fear and timidity, but of power, love, and self-discipline." Stand strong, stand confident and make forever impacts with your life. Praying for you to have a great day! God bless you!

Love, Red

Dear you,

Greatness is achieved through our actions, not words; and we'll never achieve greatness if we never try. In our quest for greatness we mustn't underestimate the beauty and power of serving one another, but rather value it. Our character defines us. Is being there with listening ears, helping hands or simply helping meet the need of another part of your character? As Sonny Barger said, "In the end, a man's character cements his fate, good or bad." I encourage you to consistently refine who you are and teach the importance of character. It's never too late to improve; we have till death. Hebrews 13:1 (NKJV) says, "Let brotherly love continue." and John 13:35 says, "By this all people will know that you are my disciples, if you have love for one another." Praying for God to speak to you today and for each of us to take a look at our own character; make the needed adjustments.

Love, Red

Dear you,

Don't complain if you're not willing to implement positive change. We as people need to stop being so sensitive, so grumpy and so offended at everything! If you don't like something, then do something, rather than nothing, to influence it and/or change it. You are empowered to stand for what is right and to influence the masses! If you STAY QUIET…NOTHING CHANGES; complaining doesn't fix the problem. Don't be a broken record; make a difference, but do it without complaining. Philippians 2:14–16 says, "Do everything without complaining and arguing, so that no one can criticize you. Live clean, innocent lives as children of God, shining like bright lights in a world full of crooked and perverse people. Hold firmly to the word of life; then, on the day of Christ's return, I will be proud that I did not run the race in vain and that my work was not useless." No use in complaining if you aren't willing to stand. Make it happen as you get after it today! God bless you!

Love, Red

Dear you,

Today is the beginning of new opportunities; opportunities that will require integrity to achieve! The way you respond and approach the day is yours to define. Just keep in mind that the reward of success is founded in part on integrity. It is far more of a reward at the end of the day to stand with integrity then to compromise with dishonesty; even when you face troubles you have to endure the pain in order to gain. Eliminate those doubts and fears, which only lead to weakness; you are an OVERCOMER and will achieve greatness! "Now all glory to God, who is able, through his mighty power at work within us, to accomplish infinitely more than we might ask or think" (Ephesians 3:20). Overcome and succeed! God bless you and may our week be filled with GREATNESS!

Love, Red

Dear you,

Relationships are stronger when unified with a purpose; being there for one another requires selfless actions; and relying on each other's core competencies allows a stronger chance to overcome life's many obstacles. If we could all grasp that everybody is a somebody we could eliminate the thoughts of folks being nobodies. To be valued, show value. John 3:16 says that we are all a "whosoever," which means you, YES YOU, are worthy of value! Praying for God's favor upon your day and weekend. God bless you!

Love, Red

Dear you,

Self-confidence begins inner transformation. Hold your head up, back straight, shoulders back and chest out; believe in yourself and carry on. You have been empowered to peer through the darkness of life and take action; action to triumph in all aspects of your life! Being a Leader requires confidence. Spiritually, we have been enabled to be bold, strong and successful through Him. Second Corinthians 3:7–16 teaches us about the new covenant and the boldness that comes along with the Holy Spirit. I leave you with verse 12, which says, "Since this new way gives us such confidence, we can be very bold!" I encourage you to consistently stand CONFIDENT and never doubt that you are a SOMEBODY! God bless you!

Love, Red

Dear you,

"I'll complete what I promised God I'd do!" Say it. Are you tired? God gives your soul rest. Are you in bad health, spiritually or physically? God is the ultimate Physician and Healer. Do you feel like so many are against you? God is for you. Have folks done you wrong? God is good to you; He has provided you a way to everlasting life. Are your eyes or soul filled with tears? God wipes away every tear and keeps your feet from stumbling. Is your anxiety peeked? God calms your mind and delivers you. Are you dealing with broken relationships? God is the everlasting relationship. Feel like you are chained to circumstances or aspects of life? Become His servant and be freed from the chains holding you down; Bondage is yours to break… BREAK IT IN HIS NAME. Feel alone? Walk in His presence; Psalm 116 is full of greatness. Verse 9 says, "And so I walk in the Lord's presence as I live here on earth!" So do you have a relationship with God? For without the relationship, religion is dead. God fulfills His promises and delivers you through what life throws at you; HE IS YOUR HOPE. Have you promised Him something, but yet to follow through? Say it again, "I'll complete what I promised God I'd do!" Live life, live it in His presence. God bless you.

Love, Red

Dear you,

Truth prevails. Never let temporary setbacks ingrain into your soul, convincing you that they are permanent; weather the storm and stay strong. Avoid arguing with unreasonable people; arguing only brings you down to their level. Your mental health is far more important than giving in to another's stupidity. I'm reminded of how much weather is like life. The beautiful sunny days represent the happy and fantastic times in life, the rainy days represent daily struggles and the storms represent life's obstacles. It's you who establishes the climate, or better yet, what you allow. When the sun breaks back out it reminds me that no matter the rain or storms, if we hold on and keep on we will see the sun shine once again. The key is to persevere. This is why I choose to stand and never give up on God, my family or you. Spiritually, at the end of the day, we are Soldiers of Christ. Second Timothy 2 is a great reference with solid instructions in weathering the storms of life. I leave you with verses 23–24, "Again I say, don't get involved in foolish, ignorant arguments that only start fights. A servant of the Lord must not quarrel but must be kind to everyone, be able to teach, and be patient with difficult people." Stay encouraged and keep that throttle of life twisted; pushing through life's storms. May your troubles be less, your blessings be more and nothing but happiness come through your door. God bless you.

Love, Red

DEAR YOU

Dear you,

Truth is simple; lies are complex. Leaders, strive to unite rather than deceive or foster negligent compromise. Smooth talk and glowing words deceive innocent people; deception leads to physical, but most importantly spiritual weakness. Spiritual weakness leads to biblical compromise, which leads to physical and spiritual demise. The time is upon us as Leaders, especially Christian Leaders, to unify and strengthen up, aligning ourselves closer to God's Word, as well as together. We all fall short, but that is no excuse for us to stay wrong just because we think it works; what God thinks is what matters. In life you meet Leaders and people that rationalize or soften their boundaries and sins by padding the truth or misquoting scripture. Why? Along the way, there were Leaders and people that wanted to twist something because of interpretations, flesh or gains in popularity. This has led many religions, groups, etc.…to create gray areas so they feel justified in the flesh. The sad part is that it has been allowed to continue, which has caused divisions within many organizations, but most importantly the body of Christ. Those being lead are not seeing unity or consistency, but are seeing negative compromise; to the point that Christianity becomes a joke because the rest of the world sees no true difference. This sets up physical failure in leading folks to spiritual success. We are to be set apart as instructed in Romans 12:2 in order to properly lead; leading requires walking the talk. Paul said in Romans 16:17–18 (NLT), "And now I make one more appeal, my dear brothers and sisters. Watch out for people who cause divisions and upset people's faith by teaching things contrary to what you have been taught. Stay away from them. Such people are not serving Christ our Lord; they are serving their own personal interests. By smooth talk and glowing words they deceive innocent people." I pray for Leaders and the body of Christ to get back to proudly standing for what's right, unified and aligned to God's Word. Like my Pastor <u>Kevin McGlamery</u> says, "WE are better together." God bless you; unite and stand strong for one another.

Love, Red

Dear you,

Hope you have a super fantastic weekend; don't let the life of people pigeons still your joy and keep you covered in mess! You see, a lot of times you are surrounded by flocks of people pigeons. Like a flock of pigeons, they all fly in and make a mess of things…then they fly away leaving you with a mess to clean. Exercise your ability to endure and stand proud as you overcome the band of pigeons. I encourage you, as you enter the weekend, take time to reflect, adjust and be prepared to move forward. Yesterday cannot be undone, but you can work on today where you failed yesterday and posture yourself to make tomorrow an even stronger day. God bless you and remember, don't feed the pigeons; teach them as you lead them. "The teaching of your Word gives light, so even the simple can understand" (Psalm 119:130).

Love, Red

Dear you,

Life doesn't have to be complex. I encourage you to look at the simplicity of life and to enjoy the very things that others take for granted. Live a life of faith, you live a life of simplicity. For when we trust in our Heavenly Dad above we can live life in the essence of simplicity; He is not the author nor creator of confusion, but the God of inexplicable peace. This morning's thoughts on simplicity reminds me of 2 Corinthians 2, which is where Paul writes to the church of Corinth. Verse 12 resonates; he tells them how proud he is of them, as I am you, and tells them that his desire is to have a testimony to have behaved in the world with simplicity and Godly sincerity, not by earthly wisdom but by the grace of God. I to strive, despite the complexity that others create, to live a simplistic Godly life and encourage you to do the same. God bless you.

Love, Red

DEAR YOU

Dear you,

Start today with thinking of others instead of yourself; sincerely wrench on the areas internally that need to be tuned, allowing you to perform at top specs for the Big Picture. Be aware of the second and third order effects of your choices; you only get one real shot at life, make it one filled with actions leading to positive legacy. It's simple; live life, live it well and die right (Romans 10:9–10). God bless you.

Love, Red

Dear you,

Experienced Leaders teach from the heart and show that it's what's in the heart that enables the art of perseverance; I speak from experience. When you don't feel able…He makes you able. When you feel tired…He keeps you going. When you feel like nobody loves you… He loves you unconditionally. When you get confused and don't understand…He gives you discernment and directs you. When you say I just can't do it…He says you can do all things through Him. Do you see the difference? He always turns a negative into a positive… that's why it's so important to follow His example. Our Heavenly Dad is the essence of HOPE, Wisdom and Understanding. Romans 5:5 says, "And this hope will not lead to disappointment. For we know how dearly God loves us, because he has given us the Holy Spirit to fill our hearts with his love." God bless you as you continue to lead not only others, but yourself.

Love, Red

Dear you,

Don't let short term negative circumstances turn into a mess, which in turn can affect your long term success; for some short term actions lead to long term consequences. Walk it out; harder done than said.

Love, Red

Dear you,

Successful Leaders value unity because they appreciate it's influence and the synergy it creates in regards to the big picture; unity fosters a stronger sub-structure and gives, the parties involved, a strategic and tactical advantage. You see, when you have discord and separation you accomplish only where you directly reach or impact, meaning that you are minimizing your capabilities; when you see unity you see the strength it brings to the overall objective. I encourage you to initiate and foster team unity and to formalize partnerships that lead to the overall success of the big picture. For a moment think about the Christian culture; imagine coming together unified serving God…WOW…the impacts are amazing; like my Pastor Kevin McGlamery says, "We are better together!" You have the power to unify, choosing to make a difference. First Peter 3:8 says, "Finally, all of you should be of one mind. Sympathize with each other. Love each other as brothers and sisters. Be tenderhearted, and keep a humble attitude." God bless you.

Love, Red

DEAR YOU

Dear you,

You are an artist; the piece of art is your life. For your past has sculpted your present and your present sculpts your future; make it personal, take it personal. I encourage you to realize that what you went, or are going, through prepares you for who you are today; yes, you are allowed to remold your life sculpture. A good artist knows that nothing is wasted and is smart enough to learn, and compassionate enough to share. Spiritually, God is the artist and we are the art, meaning that when we allow Him to mold us, form us, lead us we rest in knowing that we are indeed being perfected into a master piece! "But now, O Lord, you are our Father; we are the clay, and you are our potter; we are all the work of your hand" (Isaiah 64:8).

Love, Red

Dear you,

We serve an all-powerful and delivering God. Do not be defeated, do not let bottom feeder haters rob you of your joy and do not put yourself in the position of being taken for granted. Rise up, YES, Rise up! Muster that inner drive to rise, overcome and succeed! Muhammad Ali said, "Only a man who knows what it is like to be defeated can reach down to the bottom of his soul and come up with the extra ounce of power it takes to win when the match is even." It's up to you to succeed as the victor! So drive on and do it, make it happen! Hit up Psalm 69:4–28. Live life, live it well and die right. God bless you.

Love, Red

Dear you,

"WE" must stand strong for God and country, for our beliefs and for our families. We mustn't settle for good, but GREAT! YES, BE GREAT! Right now, get up, hold your head up and tell yourself, "I am strong and will stand ready for God, Country and my family!" Joshua 1:9 says, "Have I not commanded you? Be strong and of good courage; do not be afraid, nor be dismayed, for the Lord your God is with you wherever you go." Bottom line is "WE" need to stand strong and at the ready; our country and future generations depend on it. God has blessed us with the BACKBONE to do it, so we must use it. God bless you!

Love, Red

Dear you,

Be selfless, kind and compassionate along this ride of life. A wise person knows that sometimes you have to make your life simpler in order to makes another's better; never forget where you came from and those who helped you along the way. Yes, there will be people that take your selflessness for granted, but never lose heart. Stand fast in knowing that your internal and external legacy grows stronger when overcoming adversity. I leave you with 2 Corinthians 4:16–18. "So we do not lose heart. Though our outer self is wasting away, our inner self is being renewed day by day. For this light momentary affliction is preparing for us an eternal weight of glory beyond all comparison, as we look not to the things that are seen but to the things that are unseen. For the things that are seen are transient, but the things that are unseen are eternal." God bless you.

Love, Red

DEAR YOU

Dear you,

Lie to one, you lie to all. Be self-aware of all your actions, especially in what you speak. Why? Because they reflect who you are and are watched by the masses. Speaking truth shows respect to yourself and your relationships and, most of the time, your actions affect more than just you. I leave you with a solid word found in Proverbs 12:19 "Truthful lips endure forever, but a lying tongue is but for a moment." Keep it real each step of the way. God bless you.

Love, Red

Dear you,

A cup of coffee reminds me of life. We are born (fresh cup of coffee), we grow (things added to the cup of coffee) and then we die (coffee is drank). No matter how much creamer, flavor, sugar, etc…you put in it, it's still the same base cup of coffee. It's what goes in the coffee that changes the appearance, the taste and volume. The resemblance to life is the "what" and "who" we put in our life, these two things change our appearance, change our tastes, and contribute to our legacy. I encourage you to give your coffee (your life) to God because of all He has done for you (He makes the freshest cup of coffee). Let God transform your coffee (your life) into an award-winning cup of joe. His cup of coffee never runs out and will change your appearance, tastes and life legacy. Hit up Romans 12:1–2. Praying for you and yours to have a fantastic day! God bless you!

Love, Red

Dear you,

Live wisely and wisdom will permeate your life; mock life and life will mock you. Your life journey will have you attend a dinner party at the table of Lady Wisdom, as well as Madame Whore; the time spent at either party is up to you. You see, your life is a journey, it's creating a story; a story filled with love, romance, drama, horror, action and, eventually, tragedy. However, the depth, the details, length and outcome of each chapter depends on what you allow and/or choose to compose your life substance; for it's the substance within your life, from which you draw from in order to pen to paper, that others are given to read. They read what they see. A truth that many do their best to contest as being truth is that what you choose to fill your life with, surround yourself with will be what your left with. Yes, you have the choice to fill your life with wisdom and have self-authority to choose right rather than wrong. Proverbs 9 confirms it, as it walks you through two dinner parties; one with Lady Wisdom and the other with Madame Whore. Lady Wisdom represents God's substance; Madame Whore represents the world's. Just remember that the outcome of Lady Wisdom's party has the substance for you to write an everlasting life story, whereas Madame Whore's guests have stories that end up in hellish tragedy, forever tormented. The choice is yours, choose wisely.

Love, Red

Dear you,

There are those that are rich in money, but poor in character; as well as those that are rich in character, but monetarily poor. No matter how clean or nice one looks on the outside, if they are dirty on the inside…they still be dirty. Proverbs 22:1-2 says, "Choose a good reputation over great riches; being held in high esteem is better than silver or gold. The rich and poor have this in common: The Lord made them both." So, as the streets are hit hard with our soul, we must each strive to create and maintain a good reputation founded on clean character; be that "go to" person known to have a rich and solid Legacy. Clean on the inside by the Holy Spirit washes away the grime on the outside. God bless you!

Love, Red

Dear you,

Let's keep it real and talk about two words; transparent and agenda. The word transparent has many definitions; one being, honest and open…not secretive. Agenda is defined as a plan or goal that guides someone's behavior and is often kept secret. Hidden agendas are like a flesh-eating disease to a Nation and wind up hurting more than just you; yes, they usually end up causing pain. In this life it's best to have a legacy of transparent honesty with your Brothers. With God, respect for this principle is imperative…His life and Word are a solid example of it, which means we should follow it. In fact, we know what His agenda still to this day is, which we are to emulate, Luke 19:10 says, "For the Son of man is come to seek and to save those who are lost." Transparent and an Honest Legacy; get after it.

Love, Red

Dear you,

Life brings about metaphorical chains, at times, leaving scars. The harsh truth is, at times, you are your worst enemy; you allow the chains to get tighter and tighter, metaphorically digging and cutting deeper into your soul, which causes you to internally bleed. What makes it worse is that, externally, you appear fine, but internally are dying a slow and painful death. Even if you don't want to allow others to see your pain, God sees it; the best part is that He can fix it. I don't want you, and you don't have to, ride out life in turmoil, there is HOPE. Really? Yes, really! Allow Him to break your chains, allow Him to ease your pain, allow Him to use His scars to remove yours. Be set free through Him. "Therefore, if the Son makes you free, you shall be free indeed," John 8:36. God bless you!

Love, Red

You hungry? Each of us have entrees (life issues) on our plate ready to eat, process and digest. How we process and digest them have similarities, but each are independently different, leaving self-evaluation so important. For, it's through self-evaluation you reach an understanding of how to digest your life entree and/or curb your appetite. Yes, it's important to curb your appetite, because some things just aren't needed in your life or are too hard to process and/or digest. Just remember, there are no returns in life; once you order up your entree you have to dive right in one bite at a time. The good news is that you have control over some of the things you order from life's menu; after-all, you are the one ordering. God's menu is full of nourishment; Jesus says in John 6:35, "I am the bread of life; whoever comes to me shall not hunger, and whoever believes in me shall never thirst." So, consider the menu from which you order; make your life entree fulfilling and favorable, easy to process and digest. God bless you and be careful what you order up; eternity is at stake.

Love, Red

DEAR YOU

Dear you,

Your life makes a difference; yes, your life impacts! Even if people don't tell you, or on the days you don't feel it, you're influencing others through the consistency of your actions. Your life goes beyond exterior; your actions show what's in your heart, which is what people grow to love! This is why you must guard your heart, so, as your life rolls on, your actions match your words, which directly influences the impacts of your life. A solid Proverb in 4:23 says, "Guard your heart above all else, for it determines the course of your life." God bless you and I pray that today is your day to positively impact the life of another. It starts with you.

Love, Red

Dear you,

Don't be caught shrouded by the cloak of insanity, living as if there is no hope. FREEDOM can be more than a DREAM; peer through the darkness and take action. Don't just talk about living your dream, you have to hold your head up, lean forward and make that sucker come true. Edgar Allen Poe said, "Deep into that darkness peering, long I stood there, wondering, fearing, doubting, dreaming dreams no mortal ever dared to dream before. Those who dream by day are cognizant of many things which escape those who dream only by night." If you choose to stay quiet and simply walk away, then you are insane and have no hope in fulfilling your dreams and will only obtain mundane. Don't be part of a horrible sanity led by dreamless folks destined for insanity. When you face the horrible… Destroy it and triumph at making your dreams reality. Get out there from under the shrouded dark cloak and triumph! If you choose to let your dreams go, don't be dumbfounded when your dreams are pounded!

Love, Red

Dear you,

Sorrow is inevitable in life… It's simply part of the ride; just make sure you're suffering for the right reasons and the RIGHT cause. 1st Peter 4:12–19 is a solid passage. Pay attention to verse 19, "So if you are suffering in a manner that pleases God, keep on doing what is right, and trust your lives to the God who created you, for He will never fail you." The point is that standing for God, your family, your children and your circles will, at times, cause suffering, but you mustn't waiver on truth or God. Rise up for RIGHT! Pray for me as I pray for you. God bless you.

Love, Red

Dear you,

Life continues; get up and declare the fantastic gift of breath, of sight, of hearing and never forget God's grace! Don't let the stresses of life keep you down; you have the authority to rise up and defeat it! Yes, I know we all would love to take a break from life, but we can't. Why? Because being grown means fulfilling grown people responsibilities. What should you do? Add more Jesus to your life and be more positive in your outlook! If God's not in the center of your life, put God in it and watch the things yet to come! Romans 8:31 says, "What shall we say about such wonderful things as these? If God is for us, who can ever be against us?" So, as you get after this thing called life, exercise your Jesus authority to victoriously overcome life's stressful obstacles! Praying for you and yours to have a solid day! God bless you!

Love, Red

DEAR YOU

Dear you,

Time continues; you can't stop or rewind the clock. It's what you do within each tick and tock of the clock that determines how well your life of faith rocks. Will your life legacy talk throughout the ages of time or end up broken like an idle and torn up clock that's no longer able to chime? The choice is yours. Pick the right flock and you will produce a legacy of faith worthy to rock your life's clock. Philippians 4:13 says you can do it through the help of the one who is the master of all clocks. So, what time is it?

Love, Red

Dear you,

Even though life gets shaky from time to time, embrace the shakes and wobble with it, as you dance your faith through it. Inner joy allows your inner dance of faith to step it out. Let nothing, I repeat nothing, rob you of your joyful journey. Philippians 4:4–8 is a solid hip pocket reference to keep close to your heart. I leave you with 4–5, "Always be full of joy in the Lord. I say it again—rejoice! Let everyone see that you are considerate in all you do. Remember, the Lord is coming soon!" So, go ahead and rock that beautiful smile, bounce with it, lean with it and rock with it! Now you get after it; allow your faith to strengthen your joy as you make those gains! God bless you!

Love, Red

Dear you,

Pray, laugh, live, and love, as you get after it today. Simply be dedicated and follow through in all things. Tom Wilson once said, "A smile is happiness you'll find right under your nose." So, smile! Romans 5:8 contains one of the best reasons to smile. Even when you feel alone, God loves you and is always with you. He even helps you follow through with whatever you stay dedicated to do. God bless you today.

Love, Red

Dear you,

Be a renegade; a renegade in pursuit of positive change in your life, as well as within your circles. Be wise in your choices, for wisdom is something you continuously pursue and will empower your decision making. In fact, a solid Proverb found in 24:5 says, "The wise are mightier than the strong and those with knowledge grow stronger and stronger." Remember, you're the only one that can improve you, but when you do, you have the knowledge and wisdom to influence those around you by simply being you, which is why you must stay at your best in order to influence the rest. So, as you get after this week and those gains, continuously seek wisdom, apply knowledge and influence others! God bless you!

Love, Red

DEAR YOU

Dear you,

Not all dirt is good dirt, but some dirt is composed of the right stuff allowing it to be used as solid ground. For example, most foundations are founded on dirt; it's the type of dirt that determines the strength of the foundation. But it's not just the foundation that matters, it's the surrounding dirt. For example, the foundation's dirt can be solid but the surrounding dirt could be full of chert dirt, which prevents the site from being able to perc. Proper site evals hinge on the ability of the surrounding dirt having the ability to absorb and renew the wastewater and rain water flowing away from the foundation. This is like our life. We came from the dirt and will return to the dirt, so our foundation is made up of earthly dirt. Yes, we all have sin (some type of dirt), but, when our dirt (our life) is composed of God, we are able to maintain a solid foundation, a foundation built on solid ground. However, we can't just stop at the foundation, we have to evaluate the dirt surrounding us and still within us so that we can properly eval our ride of life to make sure our life is able to perc; meaning that we are surrounded by the right dirt so that we remain able to absorb, apply and reuse the life changing spiritual water flowing directly from our foundation, which is strongest when built on God. Psalm 51:10 says, "Create in me a clean heart, O God. Renew a loyal spirit within me." Is your dirt composed of the right stuff, or are you full of chert dirt…needing to be refined?" I encourage you to wrench in the areas needed to maintain the proper spiritual perc, so that your dirt consistently works and your foundation never fails!

Love, Red

Dear you,

A lesson learned is worth a lesson shared. How many times have you offended someone, or been offended? How many times have you held onto a grudge, losing friendships? It's sad but is a fact of life that things like this happen. In fact, a solid Proverb found in 18:19 says, "An offended friend is harder to win back than a fortified city. Arguments separate friends like a gate locked with bars." Then in verse 24 it says, "There are friends who destroy each other, but a REAL friend sticks closer than a brother." This friend is Jesus. Don't you want friends like that? Well, as you press on through this life, strive to be this type of friend; a friend modeled after Jesus. Why? Being there for one another is so important. I love the message version of Philippians 2:1–4, which I leave with you, "If you've gotten anything at all out of following Christ, if His love has made any difference in your life, if being in a community of the Spirit means anything to you, if you have a heart, if you care—then do me a favor: Agree with each other, love each other, be deep-spirited friends. Don't push your way to the front; don't sweet-talk your way to the top. Put yourself aside, and help others get ahead. Don't be obsessed with getting your own advantage. Forget yourselves long enough to lend a helping hand." The point? I encourage each of us to step out of our comfort zones and be there for one another each step of the way in any way we can be, as a friend modeled after Christ. God bless you!

Love, Red

Dear you,

Your actions and attitude, as a leader of team or self, are teaching someone how, or how not, to lead. Are they learning to lead from the front, or hide in the back? Are they seeing an arrogant leader, or a leader that leads with honorable humbleness? You must take ownership of your actions, eliminate arrogance, remain humble and adapt where needed in order to be a leader worthy to lead the way. John C. Maxwell once said, "A leader is one who knows the way, goes the way, and shows the way." "Finally, all of you should be of one mind. Sympathize with each other. Love each other as brothers and sisters. Be tenderhearted and keep a humble attitude." - 1st Peter 3:8. Stay humble, lead strong. God bless you.

Love, Red

Dear you,

Don't complain, bring the solution. As we each face this week head on, let's remember that complaining fixes nothing; yet we see it every day. If you're in the middle of a situation generate a solution, take the initiative to take action and become a mentor, an example of how to overcome, rather than a complainer. Philippians 2:14–16 is a solid hip pocket reference; apply these, sit back and watch the results generated directly through your solutions. Praying for you each to have a solid week. God bless you. Remember…don't complain, bring the solution.

Love, Red

Dear you,

You know, in life, sometimes you simply want to throw your hands up and quit; DON'T! When you throw your hands up, remember the hands of Jesus spread out and nailed on the cross. Yes, life is tough sometimes, but not tougher than Jesus hanging there for you. The eternal love of Jesus is waiting on you; waiting for you to throw your hands up to Him, as he wraps His arms around you.

Love, Red

Dear you,

It's not just in our strongest moments, but also in our weakest, where we have the opportunity to show the strength of our faith and character. Faith, even when you're down, allows your inner strength to consistently put the needs of your Brother and Sister in the forefront of your prayers and actions. Lifting them up is part of your duty; create a forever legacy, a legacy defined in part by how selfless you truly are. Words are cheap; actions…priceless.

Love, Red

Dear you,

NEVER GIVE UP! In the midst of your deepest darkest moments, if you focus, you can see the light; it's critical that in those deepest darkest times to be encouraged and to reach out, because even the smallest spark illuminates a path. Don't let those moments of darkness consume you! Your life is so important, whether you think it or not! You matter to me, but most importantly to GOD. Follow the light of Jesus to new and better days; your future is worth it! John 8:12 says, "Jesus spoke to the people once more and said, 'I am the light of the world. If you follow me, you won't have to walk in darkness, because you will have the light that leads to life.'" YOU'RE NOT ALONE! YOU, yes YOU, have value and YOUR life matters; cherish it. God bless you and may you allow His light to shine bright in yours. NEVER GIVE UP!

Love, Red

Dear you,

It's far more of a reward to stand, passionately, with integrity then to compromise with dishonesty. Don't you agree? I mean, sometimes, you might just wish you could knock this principle into people from time. However, change takes passion, so be the instrument of change and the example of what it means, to not only have, but to demonstrate integrity. Remember, we each face ladders of life; just like a strong ladder must have solid rungs that will withstand the amount of weight placed upon the climber, successful leadership must be built with integrity in order for their actions to match their words along the climb. A solid Proverb found in 10:3 says, "People with integrity walk safely, but those who follow crooked paths will be exposed." So, keep your legacy solid; don't let it be caught, metaphorically, naked. God bless you.

Love, Red

Dear you,

Life brings trials; God gives deliverance. Life brings tests; God gives you the knowledge to pass the tests. Life brings negative circumstances; God gives you the strength to rejoice. Life simply brings it; however, God gives it and empowers you to get through it. The more you overcome the stronger your heart grows. When you have the heart to fight and persevere, everything you have is worth it. I encourage you to thank God for all of His gifts and to smile at life as you get after it, while overcoming what life brings with it. "Rejoice in the Lord always: and again I say, Rejoice" - Philippians 4:4. Live life, life it well and die right.

Love, Red

Dear you,

Stop complicating simple things and don't be afraid to take back your life. Up to you to define it…own it…and grow it. Many dream of a better life. Some even imagine it, with all the possible newness and excitement. However, few lack the passion to believe it. If you dream or imagine it, then passionately implement it. Just remember, moving forward with change is far better than going backwards to shame or pain. As Johnny Paycheck said, "You know, Lord, I'm not perfect; some even call me no count, but I'll tell you: I believe a man is judged by what's in his heart…" So what's in your heart? Got passion? My passion to be the Brother that never gives up on another got stronger when I implemented Romans 10:9–10; I encourage you to do the same. I pray for God's favor to be upon you and may your stain of pain be forever gone, because you're worth it to me!

Love, Red

DEAR YOU

Dear you,

We've all had that one shirt, rag, etc…that gets stained and/or tattered beyond repair. These stains are so prevalent that there are all types of products that claim to remove the stain or protect your items from wear and tear; I can even hear that commercial in my head, "But wait…there's more!" However, they all have that one caption, "Results may vary" "Will not protect from normal wear and tear." Isn't this like life? We all have stains in life that have bled into our hearts. We all have or will experience some type of torn or tattered life event. Yes, many comparisons can be made, but there is no comparison to the best product that has been on the market for all time; that stain, chain breaking, life changing product named Jesus. The results are time tested and elimination of life and heart stains are guaranteed. His 66 love letters contain over a 100+ references of being made pure, being protected, having a refuge no matter your past, no matter your brokenness, no matter your pain. He cleans, washes, forgives and makes you new…if you let Him. Let His everlasting product cover you from head to toe, inside and out. God bless you!

Love, Red

Dear you,

This life is full of processes. Here's my take on one, which is the process of attitude. Attitude influences thoughts. Thoughts influence decisions. Decisions lead to choices. Choices lead to actions. Actions lead to consequences; consequences you are left to process. That's why it's so important to keep your attitude in check before it causes something or someone to wring your neck. You have been enabled with the power to control your attitude, which means you have the power to influence the resulted consequence. Spiritually, Colossians 3:10 says, "Put on your new nature, and be renewed as you learn to know your Creator and become like Him." So, how's your attitude looking? Is it contributing to the legacy you want left? Or are you riding down a road that leads to lots of hurt? Up to you to take control of your attitude. God bless you.

Love, Red

Dear you,

Stand up, get up and rock that smile. Let your smile become contagious! Don't let stress control you, but rather punch it straight in the mouth, declaring that today is going to be one of your best days yet! Remember, for every action is an equal and opposite reaction, which means doing your part in providing positive actions in order to yield positive reactions. In fact Matthew 7:12 says "Do to others whatever you would like them to do to you…" Now, this verse isn't about vengeance, but about love. I encourage you to think before you speak and never lose that smile, even in the face of adversity, because you, YES YOU, have the power to make a difference; plus it confuses your enemy!

Love, Red

DEAR YOU

Dear you,

Life is like a large field, filled with tall blades of grass and thickets along the way; you don't know what lies ahead until you begin to forge a way, cutting through blade by blade, thicket by thicket. Just like making a way through the blades and thickets require action, life requires yours. You have to press forward and grind through the obstacles with your head held high, shoulders back, confidently pushing through in order to obtain your dreams. You never know what is possible if you fear what lies beyond the metaphorical blades and thickets. Don't worry, you don't have to forge the path on your own; God is with you if you let him lead you. I leave you with Proverbs 3:6 which says, "Seek His will in all you do, and He will show you which path to take." I pray for you as you cut through the metaphorical fields along your ride of life. Here for you.

Love, Red

Dear you,

My heart is full of hope for you and I choose to never give up on you; so, don't let the shame of your past, or present, cripple you into believing that you have no hope. Believe that your life revolution is here and now. A great lyric from Hawk Nelson, written as God talking, says, "If you could count the times I'd say you are forgiven it's more than the drops in the ocean. Don't think you need to settle for a substitute; when I'm the only love that changes you." God loves you so much He sent His Son to die so that you may be forgiven. I encourage you to begin your life changing revolution and smile in the face of adversity, as you stand, knowing that you are indeed forgiven and that HOPE is alive in your life! YES IT IS! God's not dead and neither are you; make a difference in your life through Him, which will in turn spark that life revolution of hope and forgiveness in others. God bless you and be proud to be you, as you throttle through this thing called life.

Love, Red

Dear you,

The brown recluse is stealthy and often goes unnoticed because the initial bite is painless, but, as time goes on, it begins to poison you; destroying you cell by cell. If not treated it can lead to loss of limb, or worse case, death. You know what? Sin is like a brown recluse. At first, some sin seems innocent and goes unnoticed, but then it adds up and delivers a bite; delivering that deadly poison of a life gone astray. If sin is left untreated, the poison will internally destroy, little by little, everything you ever worked for; the integrity of your walk will be compromised. So, what can you do to stomp out the brown recluses of sin in your life? Clean yourself up, get rid of the sin. 1st John 1:9 says, "If we confess our sins, He is faithful and just to forgive us our sins and to cleanse us from all unrighteousness." So, yes, if God promises it, He fulfills it. I love you and am praying for God's favor upon your life. Just remember…only one is perfect and that is Him.

Love, Red

Dear you,

Author Nicholas Sparks once said, "You're going to come across people in your life who will say all the right words at all the right times. But in the end, it's always their actions, not words that matter!" That's spot on, especially in this life; hence the importance to say what you mean and do what you say. Live life, live it well and die right; maintain wisdom in order to build your legacy on truth and honor by acting out your word. Why? Because at the end of the day all you're left with is your word, don't let your lack of actions cause it to go bankrupt.

Love, Red

DEAR YOU

Dear you,

Stand up without compromise. Standing for what's right isn't always the most popular stand to take, but to stand without compromise is less painful than a destructive fall. However, many will waiver, becoming unstable, for the sake of those around, trying to maintain some type of image; to the point that some care more about their worldly image versus their Jesus image. Guess what? Jesus is ALWAYS around; people come and go. So, what's more important? For me, my Jesus image, because when that's right…even my worldly image falls into place…right where it should be! The Bible calls us to be set apart and stable. James 1:8 says, "A double minded man is unstable in all his ways." I encourage you to stand without compromise and maintain Jesus stability in order to prevent life's unstable falls. God bless you, I love you and am praying for you and yours to have a fantastic week!

Love, Red

Dear you,

Be happy, stay solid and stand STRONG. Quit being down on yourself and shut down the internal self-pity party. No one can steal your joy unless you let them. Yes, it's hard to remember that, but you control your emotions! The moment you lose your joy, because of someone else's actions, is the moment you just gave them control over you; may it never be! Spiritually say this one line from an old song, "I love you Lord and I lift my voice to worship you…oh my soul rejoice!" Now get out there and get after it! Joy and happiness are yours to have.

Love, Red

Dear you,

Reflecting allows you to evaluate second and third order effects of decisions made, which enables you to tighten up your lean or throttle out of a negative life curve. To reflect is wise; to deflect is foolish and can lead to unwanted impacts. Adjustments can be suggested but can only be made by you.

Love, Red

Dear you,

Many highways and byways are traveled along this ride of life; sometimes we end up on broken roads or dead ends. We may not understand the who, what, where or why some roads end up broken, but we throttle through those curves, twists and turns. Sometimes those broken roads strengthen us, allowing others to see God through the way we throttle through the curve, through the way we stay upright and/or how we get back up if we come crashing down. The key is that we are not meant to always understand the who, what, where or why, but are meant to trust that God does indeed have a plan. Isaiah 55:8-9 says, "My thoughts are nothing like your thoughts," says the Lord. "And my ways are far beyond anything you could imagine. For just as the heavens are higher than the earth, so my ways are higher than your ways and my thoughts higher than your thoughts." So, as you continue your ride of life, keep it throttled on the narrow and allow those you encounter along the way to see God in the ways you maneuver through your life.

Love, Red

DEAR YOU

Dear you,

First impressions impact the introduction. Relationships are personal in nature and usually begin with an introduction. Most of the time this personal, yet simple, introduction bridges the gap allowing another great relationship to grow. However, there are those that do not like change, they may tolerate, but never accept the relationship. Now, relate this to your relationship with Jesus. You already know Him, you introduce Him, some accept Him, yet, some reject Him. The point? Your relationship with Jesus is personal in nature, yet is worthy to be introduced to those you encounter along your ride of life. I encourage you to be cognizant of your actions; be at the ready to introduce. Why? First impressions impact the introduction. John 1:10–13 is a great hip pocket reference. God bless you!

Love, Red

Dear you,

Pay attention...a lot of folks you encounter are troublemakers that set out to ruin your life by spreading, or planting, lies about you. Proverbs 16:28 says, "A troublemaker plants seeds of strife; gossip separates the best of friends." How do you shut them down? Well, does what you say match what you do? Do what? It's so important for others to see that what you say you do is what you do; so, if they hear something negative or a lie about you, they will know that it's a lie because they see that what you do doesn't match what they hear. Did you catch it? What you do doesn't match what they hear, because they see that what you do matches what you say, which directly shuts down a liar and gossip. Yes, your actions, enable the ability to shut them down; the truth prevails. I encourage you to mean what you say and for your actions to reflect what you do. Your legacy and life require you to do your part in stomping out unnecessary slander, drama and gossip. God bless you and I pray that your holiday week is fantastic and full of truths instead of lies. Live life, live it well and die right.

Love, Red

Dear you,

Sometimes we allow situations, family, jobs or simply life to become giants in our lives; leaving us down trodden making it hard to smile. However, as one of God's children, there is always hope, and always a reason to smile; after all, we are blessed with His grace, mercy and forgiveness. Now smile! Why? Because you are resilient! Believe that no giant, situation or life is bigger or greater than the joy found in Him. I find that applying Philippians 4:4, "Rejoice in the Lord always; again I will say, Rejoice leads to a solid path!" God bless you and show others the way. Live life, live it well and die right!

Love, Red

Dear you,

When you make it through a situation, consider it grace not luck; but be careful to never misuse the power of God's grace. Be wise in all endeavors, stand on solid ground and allow the presence of the Lord, knowing that He is the rock upon which you stand, to empower and increase your wisdom. Psalm 26:8 reads, "I love your sanctuary, Lord, the place where Your glorious presence dwells." I encourage you to let today be the day you seek the Lord and begin to be wise in all aspects of your life; for there is HONOR in that! Remember, as Proverbs 26:1 says, "Honor is no more associated with fools than snow with summer or rain with harvest." Live life, live it well, and die right. Praying for you to have a solid week. God bless you.

Love, Red

Dear you,

Don't let stress, fear, anxiety or procrastination stand in your way of success; you are stronger than that. Pay attention to detail and build your reputation! As a child of God, remember that you aren't just showing your ethics or character to fellow humans, but are working to show that your ethics, character and reputation are in line with His Word. In fact, Colossians 3:17 says, "And whatever you do or say, do it as a representative of the Lord Jesus, giving thanks through him to God the Father." I challenge you to be that "attention to detail" person and to always do your best, not simply for your fellow humans, but for God. God bless you!

Love, Red

Dear you,

Risk. Esmé Bianco once said, "You can't get anywhere in life without taking risks." Sounds legit, sounds simplistic; but in reality most avoid the risk, stick with the sure things and die with the question, "What if?" You have to be bold in life in order to continue on the quest of movement, excitement and growth. Boldness requires risks! Spiritually, we experience the boldness of Peter and John in Acts 4. They spoke with boldness in the name of Jesus, they didn't compromise, despite the risk of jail. They took the risk for the right reason. I encourage each of us to be bold, eliminate fears and take the risks in making our life a life full of success. If the right risks are taken at the right time for the right reason you have the chance to eliminate the question "What if?" Whatever the risks, realize that nothing done for God is ever wasted! God bless you!

Love, Red

Dear you,

Don't let others drive you mad, nor let false accusations prove to be true. Reflect back on Alice in Wonderland. Remember, the tea party with the Mad Hatter and March Hare? Chaos at its best! You will come across many that do indeed represent both the Mad hatter and March Hare in your life; as well as someone, like the Queen of Hearts, figuratively shouting, "Off with their head!" How do you overcome the madness? Stay calm and in control. Be wise, never a fool, and overcome by diligently and responsibly doing your part to stay focused. Simply leave your haters with a smile, like the Cheshire Cat, "Now you see me; now you don't." But, just like movie sequels, you will have multiple situations that repeat themselves with similar circumstances. You can, yes you can, overcome each one and enjoy every step of the way, as long as you stay in control. This is spiritually relevant, seeing as how we were left with a solid Proverb in 29:11, "Fools vent their anger, but the wise quietly hold it back." Think on that and wear the proper hat. God bless you!

Love, Red

Dear you,

What you do today impacts your tomorrow. H. Jackson Brown, Jr. once said, "The best preparation for tomorrow is doing your best today." So, be at your best in whatever it is you do, in whatever job you have and in whatever situations you face; influence your tomorrow by fully living today. Just make sure, along this ride of life, you don't lead yourself to becoming an idle pendulum; for an idle pendulum accomplishes nothing but being an idle decoration in a broken clock. God bless you as impact life!

Love, Red

Dear you,

Think about a pool; it gets cleaned to keep it safe and presentable. Reminds me of our walk with Christ; we get clean by that life changing forgiveness, empowered by the King of Kings, which keeps our walk stronger and safer from those wild temptations the devil throws our way. Is it time for a cleansing? His forgiveness is here for you. Don't let the dirt of life pile up and destroy your heavenly walk.

Love, Red

Dear you,

Never give up hope! When you don't feel able…God makes you able. When you feel tired…He keeps you going. When you feel like nobody loves you…He loves you unconditionally. When you get confused and don't understand…He gives you discernment and directs you. When you say I just can't do it…He says you can do all things through Him. Do you see the difference? He turns a negative into a positive…that's why it's so important to follow His example. He is the essence of HOPE, Wisdom and Understanding. In fact Romans 5:5 says, "And this hope will not lead to disappointment. For we know how dearly God loves us, because he has given us the Holy Spirit to fill our hearts with his love." God bless you as you maintain your strength in hope!

Love, Red

Dear you,

Stay 3D; determined, dedicated and dependable. Let positivity be founded and grounded in your soul, as it radiates to all those you encounter along the way! Growth requires Self-Growth, which directly requires your involvement. You are worth it, John 3:16 says so. So, be at your best wherever you are in this thing called life and let your light shine! God bless you and have a fantastic day!

Love, Red

Dear you,

Firm life foundations must be built. When you generate, both, internal and external success you add value; you overcome obstacles by staying strong and focused. Continue to rise up, self-motivate and keep building that legacy, don't stop. Let the haters hate while you motivate! As one of God's, your victory is through Him as found in Deuteronomy 20:4, "For the Lord your God is He who goes with you to fight for you against your enemies, to give you the victory." The point? Let nothing stand in the way of building a firm life foundation. Live life, live it well and die right! God bless you!

Love, Red

Dear you,

Use your intelligence today! Seek knowledge and be quick to hear before you speak; do your part to prevent negative situations. Why? Proverbs 18:15 "An intelligent heart acquires knowledge, and the ear of the wise seeks knowledge." Just remember that your actions and tongue can get you into a lot of trouble; stay wise and think about Proverbs 18:21 "Death and life are in the power of the tongue, and those who love it will eat its fruits." God bless you.

Love, Red

Dear you,

Cruel people are in every walk of life; don't be one. What bothers me are the leaders that have the knowledge but wave it around because of the power it brings, rather than sharing the knowledge as a means to strengthen the team. If you want to see the character of someone give them the power of knowledge and see how they handle it. I encourage you to be a leader worth emulating; a leader that grows rather than mows down the team. Bruce Lee famously said, "Knowledge will give you power, but character respect." Spiritually, a solid Proverb found in 2:10 says, "for wisdom will come into your heart, and knowledge will be pleasant to your soul." Be wise in life and how you handle the knowledge gained. God bless you.

Love, Red

Dear you,

Never forget the power of Jesus' death, burial and resurrection. He was beat down but not beaten. He was whipped but not destroyed. He was mocked but not silenced. He was murdered, but not killed... for He rose from the pits of death. He did this for you and me; He took all the filthy sin so we could be made pure. If you don't know Him, apply Romans 10:9–10 which reads, "If you openly declare that Jesus is Lord and believe in your heart that God raised him from the dead, you will be saved. For it is by believing in your heart that you are made right with God, and it is by openly declaring your faith that you are saved."

Love, Red

About the Author

Red Kerusso is a disabled veteran, motivational speaker, leader, and writer. No matter the platform, he is very dynamic and cross functional in creating the synergy needed to foster the best in everyone. He is a husband, father, and holds a master's degree from the Florida Institute of Technology, as well as a bachelor's degree from Faulkner University. He is noted for being like King David, a man after God's own heart and is widely known for recognizing the somebody, even those that are considered a nobody, in everybody. Legendarily known for his quote "Be at your best to influence the rest!" Bottom line is that he has a gift of seeing, and ultimately, pulling out the best in everyone he encounters. His writings inspire readers at all levels.

CPSIA information can be obtained
at www.ICGtesting.com
Printed in the USA
FFHW021733020319
50803166-56225FF